NEVER LOOK BACK

Harry Crawford
June 2020

NEVER LOOK BACK

Harry Crawford

ryelands

First published in Great Britain in 2020

Copyright © Harry Crawford 2020

All rights reserved. No part of this publication may be reproduced, stored in a retrieval system, or transmitted in any form or by any means without the prior permission of the copyright holder

British Library Cataloguing-in-Publication Data
A CIP record for this title is available from the British Library

ISBN 978 1 906551 47 6

RYELANDS
Halsgrove House,
Ryelands Business Park,
Bagley Road, Wellington, Somerset TA21 9PZ
Tel: 01823 653777   Fax: 01823 216796
email: sales@halsgrove.com

Part of the Halsgrove group of companies
Information on all Halsgrove titles is available at: www.halsgrove.com

Printed and bound by Parksons Graphics Pvt Ltd, India

Contents

	Preface	7
1.	Beginnings	9
2.	School Days	19
3.	The War Years	28
4.	Joining the Indian Army, 1946	41
5.	Sandhurst	47
6.	School of Military Enginering – Chatham, 1949	52
7.	No. 1 Training Regiment RE – Malvern, 1949	55
8.	School of Military Engineering – Chatham, 1950	59
9.	32 Assault Regiment RE, 1951	61
10.	Fortress Engineer Regiment – Gibraltar, 1953-57	66
11.	Officer Cadet Squadron RE – Chatham, 1956	75
12.	School of Military Survey – Newbury, 1958	77
13.	42 Survey Engineer Regiment – Cyprus, 1960	84
14.	Headquarters Middle East Land Forces – Cyprus, 1961	87
15.	Ordnance Survey Scottish Region – Edinburgh, 1964	93
16.	42 Survey Engineer Regiment – Barton Stacey, 1966	98
17.	US Department of Defense – Washington DC, 1969	99
18.	Headquarters Ordnance Survey – Southampton	127
19.	Retirement From the Army	128
20.	Sun Life Assurance Company of Canada	129
21.	Hosier Farming Systems Limited – Collingbourne Ducis	131
22.	Marlborough Downs Training Group – Marlborough	134
23.	Wiltshire County Council – Trowbridge	136
24.	Hanover Housing Association – Wiltshire	142
25.	The Riding for the Disabled Association – Porlock	144
26.	The Exmoor Tourist Association – Somerset	146
27.	Our Exmoor Pony Enterprise	150
28.	The Exmoor Pony Society – Somerset	156
29.	The Moorland Mousie Trust	158
30.	Downsizing	161
31.	Farming	162
	Epilogue	167

Preface

The decision to write my autobiography arose from my wish to record my life story for the benefit of my family – the facts and my thoughts about my upbringing, my school days, joining the army, the places I had been during my career in the army, and the various occupations following retirement from military service. The title *Never Look Back* stems from lots of mistakes and disappointments that occurred along the way.

People reflecting on their lives often say they wouldn't have changed anything. I don't subscribe to that. Now in my tenth decade, I find myself sifting through situations where my judgement was at fault. In hindsight, and with the experience enjoyed in later life, I could have made a much better job of things that went wrong and I find the memory of them a bit disturbing.

I was brought up in a fairly strict middle-class Methodist environment. My father, Henry Gerald Crawford, expected perfection in everything and patience was not one of his strong points. My mother, whose name was Ella Ferguson Crawford, on the other hand, had a vibrant personality and was great fun. She was a very determined person. The Second World War changed things for the Crawford family but that was the case for most families. Prior to the outbreak of war we, as a family, led a fairly easygoing existence: Father's occupation was secure; his rugby and cricket activities were important to him and my mother shared and supported his interests. In a more leisurely way they both played golf and bridge. Father was an excellent bridge player while mother was very good. Father, being a keen Ulster Unionist, joined the Territorial Army in 1937 without hesitation. His loyalty to the Crown, shared by a great many veterans south of the border, was not shared by a majority in Ulster, where conscription was not in force. His service through Dunkirk, North Africa (First Army), and Italy saw him decorated for bravery by both the British government and the American administration but ended with devastating wounds, many years in hospitals, and ultimately confinement to bed at home for the last years of his long life.

My joining the Indian Army from school was quite accidental, reflecting a total absence of career planning, a failure on the part of my school to prepare me for entrance to university and to encourage some vision of a future. None of this would have happened had I enjoyed my father's influence. He intended that I should read medicine at the University from which he had graduated as a civil engineer. That possibility foundered as a consequence of the war.

These were the circumstances in which I grew up and eventually prospered. It amazes me now in later life how much one remembers about the past and the details that come to mind. The process of writing triggers all sorts of memories long forgotten. It would have been easier had I thought to keep diaries, and I strongly recommend that anyone with a unique or unusual career such as mine record the details of important events in their lives.

Henry George Walker Crawford

Harry, a subaltern, Corps of Royal Engineers.

– 1 –
Beginnings

My earliest recollection is of a door allowing access to a sandy beach, the sea and a couple of islands. It is etched on my memory as a happy childhood place. It was the back entrance to the little house where we lived in Skerries, just outside Dublin.

During a visit to Skerries in the eighties, Sue and I walked the beach and found that back door, still intact. This brought back other memories, such as my mother fetching water from a pump in the street and cooking on a paraffin oil stove. While walking around the town, I recognised the Methodist church, the railway station, which had been the family's link with the outside world. I saw cousin Brian Crawford's grandmother's house, where he kept his boat, and the windmill past which Mother's help, 'Tiny', had pushed my pram many times. To Tiny, I was Wee Sari. I can't remember her surname nor why she was called Tiny, perhaps it was because she was anything but! On our visit, Skerries seemed strangely unchanged. It surprised me that I remembered so much about those early days since I couldn't have been more than four or five when the family moved to Belfast.

Rugby football was one of Father's greatest interests during the whole of his life, an interest shared by the whole Crawford family. His brother Ernie had played the round ball until twenty-four and thereafter rugby for Ireland thirty times as captain of the Irish side fifteen times, eleven of them victoriously. He was appointed President of the Irish Rugby Football Union in 1958. In a tribute published in the 1 March, 1958 issue of the *Irish Times*, he was described as being among the greatest full-backs, a deadly and fearless tackler, and a fine kicker. Above all, the article said, Uncle Ernie a man who played with his intelligence throughout the game and who would never admit himself beaten.

Uncle Ernie – President Irish Rugby Football Union 1958.

There are two stories about him both mentioned in books and worthy of mention here. While driving his Daimler car towards O'Connell Bridge, following an international won at Lansdowne Road, Dublin, he bumped into a tram car. The tram driver got out of his tram, straightened his coat and approached the offending car. Uncle Ernie lowered his window and before he could utter a word the tram driver exclaimed "Agh its you Mister Craafurd, oi'll move me tram out of the way!" Ma and Pa were both in the car, also his wife, Florence.

The second incident took place during an international in Paris. The French three-quarters were advancing towards the Irish line with Uncle Ernie, at fullback, the only Irishman between the French and a certain try. He turned about, joined the French line and called "passez" whereupon one of the French three-quarters passed him the ball. He then turned and kicked it safely into touch. The French crowd roared with anger and it was said that the gendarmes had to restrain a few of them hell bent on expressing their disgust face-to-face.

Pa Crawford and a wild Irish character called Jimmy Duff were two of a number of enthusiasts who formed the Skerries RFC, using a not-very-flat meadow just outside of town. Cattle had to be chased off the ground before most matches. Like many football clubs, 'Skerries' was started on a shoestring. Pa used to talk about riding his cycle to the field in those early days, togged up and ready for play, and returning home, mud and all, for a bath.

During our short holiday in Skerries, Sue and I managed to find the site of the Skerries RFC with its smart club house. Peering through the windows, we saw a mural illustrating the Club's badge hanging on an end gable wall. The age of it and the discoloration suggested that it might well have been something original from the Crawford/Duff era. Father's farewell to the RFC included the presentation of a silver cigarette case, which he left to me, enscribed: Presented by the members of Skerries RFC to H G Crawford, December 1931.

By all accounts, Mother and Father were very happy in Skerries, so much so that mother claimed she had cried all the way in the train to Belfast when father's career involved a move. Such was her devastation on parting with dear friends and a place she loved so much.

Since graduating as a Civil Engineer at Queen's University, Belfast, Father had been employed by the Great Northern Railway (Ireland) on various assignments with a salary, he used to recall, of £400 a year. The company's tracks and bridges up and down the country included several of his achievements, some of which remain in place to this day. Two come to mind: the reconstruction of the railway bridge over the River Boyne at Drogheda and a viaduct at Bessbrook, near Crossmaglen, an area which he used to say was no place for honest men. When supervising the replacement of the bridge at Drogheda, he said he often lay awake in his digs listening to the

My father, Gerald Crawford BSc, AMICE.

BEGINNINGS

clickity-clack as the early morning trains moved slowly over the construction, in the knowledge that some parts of it were of a temporary nature.

Now Father's change of job involved leaving railway lines for tram lines. He was appointed Permanent Way Engineer, to the Belfast City Corporation, with responsibility for the city's extensive tram tracks.

Sometime later, Uncle Ernie, who had been financial officer to the Rathmines Urban Council in Dublin, was appointed City Treasurer, Belfast City Council. He lived with us for a while, and I remember his singing every morning in the bathroom. He sang hymns!

Before her marriage Mother's home was in Windsor Park, Father's in Balmoral Avenue. Ma, originally at

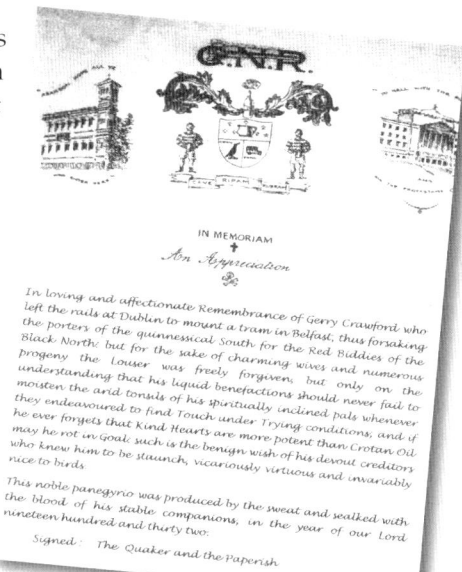

Father's career move from the GNR(I) to Belfast Corporation's Transport Department.

Mother and Father's wedding.
Front row from left: *Trixie, Joy Hurst, Pat Crawford, Rona Beck.*
Backrow from left: *Unknown, Father, Mother, George Palmer.*

Victoria College, complained bitterly to her own mother about the school and, so she said, secretly altered her school report in such a way that her suggested alternative school was considered appropriate. As a result, she joined her boyfriend, my father, as a boarder at the Methodist College.

Grandmother and Grandfather Walker were strict Scottish Covenanters. Sunday was a very quiet time at Windsor Park where the day was devoted to Bible reading and the learning of passages in the catechism. Ma chose to apply herself to the Sunday routine by 'studying' in her bedroom. During the evening there were occasions when my father gained access to her bedroom by climbing a drain-pipe to the first floor, so she said. Grandmother's footsteps on the stairs to announce supper was the signal for Pa to make a hasty retreat.

Their relationship thus developed to eventual marriage. On the Sunday prior to her marriage, the Minister at the family's Scottish church implied in his sermon that she was committing a terrible sin by marrying a Methodist! Her subsequent escape to Skerries must have been a joy for all sorts of reasons, not least the fact that she didn't like her mother much. She adored her father and, looking forward to his return each evening, removed the small change from his trouser pockets.

Grandfather Walker was a railway man. He started his long career in the GNR(I) as Station Master at Dromore, a remote country station, and worked his way up to become Traffic Manager of the company. He was a very popular figure known as 'Mr Joe' by just about everybody on the railway.

There was an interesting incident during the 'troubles' when the family lived in Dublin, before moving to Windsor Park, Belfast. Grandfather failed to arrive home from his office in Belfast. There was a knock on the front door. Looking apprehensively through an adjacent window Grandmother saw a man with a scarf around his face. Through the closed door, he advised that Mr Walker had been taken prisoner but not to fear, he would be well looked after if some sheets and blankets could be provided for the 'Cause'.

Grandfather Walker.

It transpired that instead of returning in the comfort of a First Class compartment, as was his custom, Grandfather had been on the footplate of the engine. The driver and fireman, too frightened to drive the train to Dublin

BEGINNINGS

alone, agreed to do so if Mr Joe would accompany them. On arrival at Amiens Street Station, the crew, plus Mr Joe, were arrested by the Fenians. Some days later, Grandfather returned no worse for his experience.

Comparing those times with the subsequent troubles in the '60s and '70s, Ma Crawford always claimed that the earlier troubles were honourable. Whistles were blown before the shooting in Dublin started and again when the deeds were done. Innocent folk were never targets. The 'rising' was political involving politicians only. When Grandfather died, years later, his funeral cortege paused outside Belfast's Victoria Railway Station where many employees were on hand to pay their respects.

Grandmother's family had been farmers. I remember visiting them on the odd Sunday for tea and being struck by the poor state of the farms, the farmhouses and, indeed, the relatives.

My grandmother was quite the lady among her poorer relatives. She had had three children. Uncle Percy Walker was a doctor married to Sheila Mary, and Aunt Josephine, aka Jose, was a community nurse. The third was, of course, my mother, Ella Ferguson Walker, Ferguson being Grandmother's maiden name. Jose had a son, my cousin Ronnie.

Uncle Percy had been a Medical Officer in the Royal Navy for the 1914-18 War. He was subsequently appointed Head of Belfast Corporation's Sanatorium, where he got into a great deal of trouble being accused of having an affair with the Matron and failing to account for certain financial transactions. I used to find him at the Walker's home in Cranmore Park at the end of the day telling Grandmother about his problems, all of which he denied and of which he was subsequently cleared. Uncle Percy was extremely unfriendly towards me. He used to glare at me and it occurred to me later in life that he resented everything to do with the Crawfords because of their association with the Corporation.

During the scandal involving Percy, his sisters, my mother and my aunt Jose, used to meet regularly for an update over afternoon tea at a smart restaurant called Robinson-Cleavers.

Mother was very fond of her sister Jose, who had a rotten life, having married an alcoholic and been divorced. As a community nurse, Jose was much respected by a great many people in the poorer districts of Belfast. In spite of the hostility that existed between Protestants and Catholics she was warmly welcomed wherever she went.

The Crawford grandparents lived in Balmoral Avenue, Belfast. Grandfather,

Grandfather Crawford.

who died shortly after I was born, was a commercial traveller in ladies' underwear. There were six children: Uncle Ernie, Uncle Harold, Aunt Irene (known as Girley or Gee), Aunt Trixie, Aunt Olive, and my father. Aunt Irene, an accomplished singer and music teacher, went off to India for a holiday visit to a school friend and married her friend's brother, Eric MacGregor, then an officer in the 1st/12th Frontier Force Regiment, Indian Army. Aunt Trixie became a Froebel teacher and married Barney Dickson, shortly after he qualified as a dentist. Barney really wanted to be a doctor but his father, a Methodist minister, could not afford the fees for the longer course. However, having graduated as a dentist he return-

Uncle Ernie, Aunt Olive, my father, Uncle Harold.

Aunt Trixie, my father, Aunt Irene (AKA Girley).

ed to Queen's and completed the medical degree course at his own expense. It was said that in order to subsidise his expenses he mowed the University's lawns. Aunt Olive, whom I never knew, died before I was born.

Grandmother Crawford was a dear person and very fond of my mother. I remember sitting on her knee while she sang the hymn "Jesus loves me this I know ..." Her son Ernie and Harold joined up for the First World War as private soldiers and were subsequently commissioned. They were both wounded, Harold losing a leg on the Somme.

Harold's life was saved by the devotion of a nurse whom he subsequently married. She was a Catholic and became Aunt Nan. They lived in Dublin, where Uncle Harold worked in a men's outfitting establishment. When Grandfather Crawford heard of the marriage, he apparently said it would have been better had Harold died on the Somme, a reflection of his deep animosity for Catholics and an example of the bigotry that continued to plague the chances of peace in Northern Ireland. Harold was banished from home. The day Grandfather Crawford died, Grandmother's first thought was to ask my mother to fetch Harold home.

Grandmother Crawford.

My father's uncle, Jack, was ship's surgeon on the *Rangitangi*, a liner of the Orient Line in far east waters. I met him only once before the war during a brief visit after a long absence. He had brought my sister Sheila, then about six years of age, a pretty smocked dress from Shanghai. The ship was sunk by the Japanese during World War II. Jack survived and reached a remote Pacific Island where he was later found dead.

I spent many happy holidays at the home of my Aunt Trixie and Uncle Barney in Templepatrick. Uncle Barney had a fully equipped work-

Great Grandfather and Great Grandmother Crawford.

shop, and he was a first class carpenter and joiner in his spare time, and he taught me a good deal about woodwork. His son Michael became a doctor, and his sister Jennifer, known as JJ became a physical training instructor.

Girley was a professional singer teaching singing at various schools. While teaching at Bishop's Storford in England, she suffered an embarrassment when George Palmer, my father's best friend and my Godfather, turned up unexpectedly one afternoon to enquire of the headmistress about a vacancy for a daughter he didn't have! During the course of touring the school, to Girley's astonishment, he appeared in her classroom. George was very keen on Girley and would have done well to marry her but they remained just good friends to the end of their respective days.

George Palmer and my father.

In 1939, Girley decided to visit a friend from her school days at Roedean, living with her friend's family in India. As war was imminent, sailing to India was considered a risky venture. However, off she went. In due course, she fell in love with her friend's brother, married him, and remained in India throughout the War. Hence Uncle Eric, who was a Major in the Indian Army, and subsequently Commanding Officer of the First Frontier Force Regiment. Girley drove an ambulance in India during the war, while Uncle Eric was abroad in various theatres. He was in Tobruk, North Africa, for the siege following the battle of Alemein and went on to fight the war in Burma. He ended his career as Base Commander, Lahore, in the rank of Brigadier.

On returning home at the end of hostilities, they settled in Belfast, where Uncle Eric took charge of St John Ambulance Brigade in Ireland. They had a daughter, Brigid. It was said that I was the son Girley never had such was her interest in my progress at school and subsequently when, surprise, surprise, I decided on a career in the Indian Army.

Olive, married to Alfie Hurst, died before I was born, leaving house keeper Mrs Carson to bring up my cousins Joy and Mitchell at their home, Killyheflin, on the shore of Lough Erne. The Hurst family later moved to Mount Vester, a lovely old place on the edge of Dunmurry.

On moving from Skerries, we lived in a tiny house in Bawnmore Drive,

Belfast, before moving to a three-storey terrace place in Eglinton Avenue not far from the Palmer family. George Palmer was my father's best friend, subsequently his Best Man, and later my Godfather. While I don't remember Grandfather Crawford, I have a vivid memory of my Grandmother. She was a lovely person, and my mother was very close to her, much moreso than to her own mother whom she disliked intensely. When Grandmother Crawford died, the Will required that the house and contents be sold at auction and the proceeds divided evenly amongst the surviving children. My father attended the auction and, amongst other things, bought the house, named 'Arigna' (after a coal mine in County Sligo, Ireland) in Balmoral Avenue, Belfast, where he had grown up. The telephone number was Belfast 441.

Grandmother Crawford's relatives lived in Drumshambo, County Leitrim, in the south of Ireland. The family name was Saddlier. Drumshambo was another holiday haunt for me, where I spent happy days under the strict control of Great Aunt Sarah and Great Uncle George, who were brother and sister. Their big house was above CRAWFORD'S shop in the main street, a well-known general store from which was sold all manner of things.

At 10 a.m. every weekday morning the 'Closed' sign was displayed. George and Sarah, together with the shop assistants, retired upstairs where Sarah, playing the piano and George the violin, held a short service of hymns, prayers, and a reading after which business was resumed. They were a staunch Methodist family and the cornerstone of the church in Drumshambo. The Laird family, connected to Grandmother Crawford (née Saddlier), owned a jam factory in the town, where the famous Brefney Blossom strawberry jam was produced.

There was a narrow gauge steam railway running from Roscommon, through Drumshambo, to Belturbet. One morning Sarah set off in her finery for a shopping spree, starting the journey in a pony and trap driven by George, with me beside him. On returning to the house, George noticed that Sarah had forgotten her umbrella. Off we went in the trap following the railway line running beside the road until we caught up with the train. Once abreast of the engine George waved the umbrella at the driver who brought the train to a halt. Sarah was pleased to have her umbrella.

The discovery of my deafness in one ear was revealed during a birthday party when I asked my mother where I should hide for 'Hide and Seek'. She whispered a suggestion to my left ear. I apparently said "Can't hear in that ear"! Next day, my ear was examined by father's friend ENT specialist Jim Wheeler, who pronounced my left ear stone dead. One becomes accustomed to dealing with such disabilities, but in my sixty-something year I applied for a disability pension on grounds of a deterioration of hearing, arising from noise from firing guns and from demolitions. The examination revealed a deterioration of my right ear but also that I was not totally deaf in my left year. As a result I was awarded a substantial and continuing disability pension. My only regret was that I had not made the application much earlier.

For my further education I was presented in the headmaster's study at the Friends School in Lisburn. It was, of course, a Quaker establishment not that that made any difference to Methodist me. The most exciting prospect was the opportunity of escaping from the top floor via a chute in the event of fire, as illustrated in the brochure. Once accepted as a pupil, father took me aside to delve deeply into my experiences at Malone School and the possibility that I might have heard some very bad language that would not be appropriate at Friends School. I wasn't able to help and the matter was dropped.

The transition from Malone to the fee-paying, uniformed Friends School seemed an important step with new requirements attached. One thing I found exceptionally disagreeable was the wearing of ankle socks in summer, same as the girls. The other most disagreeable aspect was homework under Father's close supervision. He was meticulous about figure work. No mistakes were tolerated. When I made mistakes, a frequent occurrence, he would get to work scraping with a razor blade after which I occasionally made another mistake in the same place. He would then explode and the result of more razor blading was a hole in the paper.

In comparison with present day teaching methods, Father's ways were atrociously discouraging. I hate to say it, but he destroyed self-confidence such was his demand for perfection. He expected more from me than I was able and I recall feeling something of a disappointment except on the rare occasions when I got things right.

– 2 –
School Days

Miss Forbes, my first teacher at Malone Public Elementary School, was a real witch. In retrospect, she was a very good teacher, but the discipline and the terror that pervaded her classroom most days was unforgettable.

The one thing she discovered I could do better than anyone else in the class was draw. There was an annual competition run by Oxo as a promotion. This entailed colouring black and white illustrations and submitting pencil drawings of favourite things. My drawing of my Elswick cycle adorned the wall of the classroom for a whole year. I have often wondered why that natural ability, which I have enjoyed ever since, failed to trigger in someone's mind the possibility that I might have made an architect.

I was a member of the scout troop attached to the Osbourne Park Methodist church, with Barry Dudgeon, the troop leader. We had tremendous fun playing all sorts of games one evening a week. On special occasions ,we would walk the 4 miles from Osbourne Park to Dunmurry and arrive at an estate off Dunmurry Lane, where we practiced for our badge tests, cooked our food on open fires, and generally had a good time before walking back home.

By way of supplementing those activities, my father, his friend Douglas Hannah, son David Hannah, and myself, went camping for a weekend. My father and Douglas, being military-minded people, aimed to keep the exercise very organized. We slept in two tents with a third as a Mess tent, outside of which was erected a flag pole. At dawn and at dusk respectively, we raised and lowered the Union Jack. There were lots of father-to-son chats during walks, and at mealtimes, the sons undertook most of the cooking and other chores.

Uncle Ernie and his family lived in Osbourne Park, where I used to go after church for Sunday dinner. Sunday school was later in the afternoon. Those were enjoyable times in Uncle Ernie's huge house. Outside, prominent gas lamp standards on the roadside indicated his position as City Treasurer. One wall in the vast billiard room displayed photographs of his rugby achievements, e.g. Ernie in action as full-back, introducing the Irish team to the King, etc.

Like many of my generation, I well remember the day in September 1939 when war was declared. It was pouring with rain as Prime Minister Chamberlain's announcement came over the wireless. My recollection of that moment was that the announcement was not unexpected. Perhaps Father's enthusiasm as a member of the Territorial Army during the previous twelve months had something to do with my acceptance of the situation. Little did we realise the impact of the war would have on our lives and circumstances. Father was then with the 3rd Battery of the 9th Searchlight Regiment TA, Royal Artillery. Not much later, he went off on an exercise, so he said.

The next we heard of him was from France where he had arrived with the British Expeditionary Force (BEF). With the fall of France, he found himself on the beach at Dunkirk. Being a good swimmer, he was able to bypass the queues for the rescue vessels and made his own way to a destroyer lying off-shore. But he had left all his possessions on the beach and swam out wearing two suits of service dress. Half way across the channel, the ship was hailed by a command vessel and ordered back to the beaches to collect more survivors there being spare room on the decks. Survival then seemed doubtful but survive he did.

I can't remember the source of the message, but we did learn that he was on his way home on the Stranraer ferry. I was appointed to meet him at Larne, and I wondered whether or not I would recognise him. But I did and he said later that he had recognised me on account of my wearing clothes which he recalled were his own, long since forgotten.

My second school was the co-educational Friends School in Lisburn. On taking me to meet Mr and Mrs Douglas, headmaster and headmistress respectively, I remember my father explaining how different it would be compared with the Malone Public Elementary School where my education had started. He was anxious to hear about the bad language I might have heard there and stressed how it would be embarrassingly unacceptable at Friends. I hadn't experienced anything bad about the school and assumed father's imagination was at work. I travelled to school on the train from Balmoral, picking up others at Derryachy, Lambeg and Hilden, and on to Lisburn.

My first girl-friend, Helen Kirk, and I sat at adjacent desks in the front row at school. Our English teacher, Marjorie McKee, made me recite a poem which started off "Helen fair, beyond compare, I'll make a garland of your hair ..." The rest of the class, well aware of my attraction to Helen, used to enjoy this when it happened, as it did on more than one occasion. The school had a Boy's Track and a Girl's Track to which the boys and girls would retire for exercise during morning breaks. I narrowly avoided a lot of trouble one day by darting down the girl's track to see Helen. Several of her girl-friends kept watch for us and the interlude passed undiscovered.

The potential for learning at Friends School was adversely affected when it was taken over and became a US Army Military Hospital, following the arrival of the Americans. We trooped around Lisburn from hall to hall when not in the Meeting House, where several classes took place at the same time amongst the pews. It was hopeless, but the staff did their best in extremely trying conditions. Not that the routine was any worse in my case than for thousands of others, but it undoubtedly interfered with the process of early learning.

I used to enjoy riding my bicycle to school. It was a 5-mile trip from

SCHOOL DAYS

Dunmurry to Lisburn, and I had it timed almost to the minute. The outward ride involved a few hills, but free-wheeling most of the way home was compensation enough. Cycling to school avoided a great deal of wasted time at the end of the school day, waiting at Lisburn Station for the train home. I recall spending hours watching goods wagons being shunted into train sets, hours when I could have been doing homework or at least some study. In retrospect, I should have worked in the Station Waiting Room.

The Queen's Hall at Balmoral became an ice rink when not in use for the annual agricultural exhibition. I taught myself to skate and in spite of many initial bumps and bruises became quite good. Good enough to justify a pair of ice hockey skates on which I would fly around the rink at great speed. Attempting to skate backwards was not very successful. My visits to the ice rink took place during evenings. The outward journey by bus from Dunmurry was easy, but getting home around 9 or 10 in the evening was tricky because the buses from the city en route to various country destinations were usually full by the time they reached Balmoral. Bus after bus would pass, but eventually one would stop and pick me up.

I didn't much enjoy once-a-week elocution classes. My mother was determined to moderate my North of Ireland accent. It wasn't really too bad and certainly never reached the distinctive and rather rough and harsh accent attributed to Belfast.

I was always able to imitate the Belfast accent, and when in Gibraltar, it was found useful during amateur dramatic productions with the Royal Navy on the cruiser HMS *Ceylon*. I did a lot of that and it was thoroughly enjoyable. Much later when in Cyprus I took over the Berengaria Players, in Limassol. Apart from keeping the group a going concern, I acted in several productions using a Belfast accent which the audiences found amusing.

In 1942, it was decided that I should leave the Friends School and move on to board at Portora Royal School, Enniskillen. Uncle Ernie knew the Headmaster, Ian Stewart, who had played rugby for England and the arrangements were made between them. In due course, Uncle Ernie took me to the school and introduced me, together with a pair of Cotton Oxford rugby boots with both tongues endorsed 'W E Crawford'! There were four houses, Leinster, Connaught, Ulster and Munster. I was placed in Munster. It was a great rugby school and although I played rugby for Munster I never achieved the perfection intended by Uncle Ernie. In retrospect, I recall the efforts of 'Frankie' Roulette, the Assistant House Master, to develop my capability on the rugby field with one-to-one tuition, but regrettably it came to nothing. Whilst enjoying the game, I failed to get selected for the school team.

However, I became interested in rowing and was gradually coached by George Andrews (French Master and House Master Ulster House) until my final year, when I was Number Two in the Portora Four, which went on to win all of the regattas in 1946 in competition with the Colraine, Limerick, Dublin, and Belfast schools.

The 1948 Portora Royal School's successful crew.

In preparation, for that most successful year the four of us spent a few days on Lough Erne, during which we rowed 56 miles before running aground adjacent to Killyheflin, formerly the home of the Hurst family and my cousins Joy and Mitchell but had since become a hotel. George, as Cox, had ventured a bit too close to the shore and holed the boat. We came to a halt with the boat on the floor and water up to our waists before retiring to the hotel where we were very well looked after.

By the end of those few days we had achieved spectacular balance and complete co-ordination, which undoubtedly paid off for our subsequent and successful tour of Ireland, after which we all won our Rowing Colours. Robin Tamplin, Number two in the boat, went on to row for Trinity College, Dublin and, I believe, rowed for Ireland in the Olympics.

Mentioning George Andrews reminds me how my French was of a pretty poor standard, so much so that he would grab my hair and bang my head on my desk as if to emphasise my feeble interpretation. My Greek wasn't much better. Micky Murphet, our classics master, occupied a very desolate classroom without a picture on the walls. I assumed this was in order to ensure his pupils would concentrate on the lesson. I well remember an afternoon under his gaze, when my Ovid was not going very well. He exclaimed, "Crawford, go to 4B." I left the class room, went to 4B classroom, and while I can't recall what was happening there, I do remember that I discontinued classical studies. It was a huge relief!

A note about George Andrews, with whom I corresponded annually, is worthy of mention. We frequently attended Old Portoran dinners together in London. George enlisted in the French Navy as a seaman for World War II, and later became commissioned. Following the German invasion of France, he found himself as a Liaison Officer on a French ship when the Royal Navy attempted to blow its opponents out of the water at Toulon. It was after his return to school mastering and through rowing that we became acquainted and good friends until his death in 1996. In 1992, he paid me a visit, staying overnight at The Dell, on his way to see his brother in Bude. While sitting in the garden, he announced that two terrible things had happened at Portora: the school had ceased to be a boarding establishment, but worse, girls were now being admitted! As a confirmed bachelor, his distaste for the latter was not surprising. As a Mason, he rose to become Grand Worshipful Master of all Ireland.

Portora Royal School was created by James I for the education of the sons of the farming community in the west of Ulster. By the time I got there, it had become a leading public school in Ireland, its chief rival being Campbell College in Belfast. Like all schools throughout the UK, it suffered on account of the war, with staff called up in the armed forces.

At Portora, one followed the day-to-day curriculum, but the notion of an education planned towards a career seemed absent. For instance, I found myself apparently prepared for the matriculation examination at Queen's University, Belfast. I say 'apparently' because there was no consultation about it, no tutorial and no explanation. On reporting for the examination, I found myself entered for French, Engineer Drawing, English, Mathematics, and Art. I staggered through the French, which was oral and totally unexpected. As for Engineer Drawing, I hadn't a clue, not having seen an engineer drawing never mind produce one. It was a total disaster due to a lack of preparedness for which, on reflection, I blame the school. I believe, also, that if one was bright, an interest was taken. If not bright, one was left to plod along. I was not bright!

During the holidays, I spent a good deal of time doing errands for Ma in Belfast. At other times, we frequently visited her great friend Kathleen Gillespie, who lived across the road in Balmoral Avenue, Betty Palmer (George Palmer's sister), and Aunt Girley (or Gee), home from India.

I was very fond of Gee, and she took a great interest in my progress – if one can call it 'progress'. Her tales of life in India were legion. I didn't realise at the time that India was going to feature in connection with my future. At other times, I stayed with Auntie Trixie and Uncle Barney, at Templepatrick. I really looked forward to those visits, largely because Uncle Barney had a workshop equipped with just about everything needed for carpentry.

Once a week, those of us who belonged to the Portora OTC (Officer Training Corps), paraded in our 1914-18 style uniforms, i.e peaked caps, tunics, knickerbockers, and roll-around puttees over boots. In the summer, we went on an annual all night exercise, which was good fun. The Regular Army came to the school for our Certificate 'A' and Certificate 'B' examinations – rifle shooting, map reading, drill, and TEWTs (Tactical Exercises Without Troops). Passing these examinations qualified us to be considered for the Army! Sometime later, and influenced by the war, an ATC (Air Training Corps) was formed. Also, a naval outfit, though I can't remember its title. Anyhow, as soon as I discovered that the boys in the ATC were paying visits to the Fleet Air Arm base at Killadeas on Lough Erne, I got myself transferred from khaki to blue.

The following summer, we went to Killadeas for a two-week camp during the holidays. We spent most of the time scooting around Lough Erne in fast moving launches, re-supplying the Sunderland and Catalina flying boats. We had turns at the helm of the boats, and on several occasions, went off flying for hours and hours out over the Atlantic in the flying boats. Once airborne, the heading was set and the automatic pilot applied. This was a bit boring, except that we had an opportunity to ask questions and explore the aeroplanes in flight.

I have a vivid memory of sitting up in the co-pilot's seat in a Sunderland when the Captain, in his seat, explained the controls before gently withdrawing the automatic pilot (a sort of fork in the floor). With my hands and feet on the controls, there was a bit of a wobble but with a little assistance, I soon managed to hold the aeroplane on a steady course and was left to get on with it. A fantastic experience for a sixteen year-old!

A Sunderland flying boat on Lough Erne.

Sunday dress was grey suits, black shoes, white shirts, and school ties. After breakfast, we would assemble for the walk to church in Enniskillen. We wore top hats and dark overcoats, if we owned them. Due to the restricted allocation of clothing coupons, without which clothes could not be bought in the North of Ireland, many of us didn't have dark overcoats. My own was brown herring bone, which with a black top hat was a sight to see and one much enjoyed by the American soldiers based in the locality. But we did deals over clothing coupons with the boys from the South, who qualified for a token issue of coupons. I recall swopping my hard-boiled egg or a tin of baked beans or whatever for a few coupons which Ma found very handy.

SCHOOL DAYS

Being of Methodist upbringing, I found myself in a croc of just five boys bound for the Methodist church. The majority went to the Church of Ireland cathedral and I soon became aware of the fun they had, especially at harvest thanksgiving when all apples decorating the pews and within reach were pocketed. One Sunday, I decided to join the cathedral croc. No one seemed bothered. I thus became a member of the Church of Ireland and was confirmed as such.

Speaking of 'church', I should mention the hours spent with Ma collecting for the Osborne Park Methodist church mission some years previously. We would have a list of the addresses of the congregation members and tour up and down the streets, roads, and parks, knocking on doors and collecting money. At the end of this exercise, Uncle Ernie would put his hand deeply into his pocket and initiate a generous increase in the total collected. His contribution was so substantial that I was paraded in front of the congregation one Sunday when the visiting Missionary pinned a medal on my chest. I was quite proud of my medal, and much later, while at Portora Royal School, I was foolish enough to display it hanging on the inside of my locker door. I say 'foolish' because from that moment on I was nicknamed 'Holy Harry' for the rest of my time at the school.

In due course, I became a Munster House Prefect and later a School Prefect. The Holy Harry title did make the process of maintaining discipline when in charge of Junior Prep somewhat difficult. They were a noisy lot and since the Prep took place in a room in the Headmaster's house, I expected him to appear at any moment. But he didn't, and I recovered control by selecting a nasty little ring-leader and sending him out as an example of what would happen to anyone else.

I took piano lessons at Portora but progress was very poor for the usual reason – lack of practice. As there were three music rooms, each equipped with a piano, my lack of interest was inexcusable. But an interest in music prevailed. I used to go down to the Steel Hall where morning assembly took place and managed to open the organ with a paper clip. I enjoyed playing the organ a great deal, so perhaps I should have been learning that instead of the piano.

The Tuck Shop was run by a chap in the town whom we called 'Rook'. He had a café at the bottom of Portora hill where we used to go for baked beans on toast when hungry and we were hungry a lot of the time. Pocket money dealt out by the House Master was one shilling per week, which didn't go very far but parents usually sent us back to school with a few bob extra. The Tuck Shop was along a lane leading down-hill to the rugby grounds.

One day, a couple of us saw an American soldier in the lane at the top of the hill. We toddled along towards him and said we were going down to the rugby grounds. Not today, he said. Next morning at Assembly the Headmaster informed everyone that General Eisenhower, Commander of the American forces, had inspected a Division on the rugby grounds as part of his preparation for the invasion of Europe. Many years later, must have been in or around 1990, the rugby grounds were named the 'Eisenhower Playing Fields' on the anniversary of the war time occasion in the presence of the American ambassador.

Another memory of the presence of American military in Fermanagh, and particularly local to Portora, was the occasion when the Headmaster invited the Commanding Officer of a US Engineer Unit to dinner. The Headmaster explained that our cricket pitches overlooking Lough Erne were on three levels and how he wished the pitch on the top level could be reduced to the level of the middle pitch, with the spoil from the top pitch spread over the lower pitch, thus raising it to the level of the middle pitch. The result would present one of the finest cricket pitches in the whole of Ireland.

It so happened that the local Engineer unit was equipped with a great many small bulldozers to be deployed on the Normandy beaches for the removal of obstacles. The Commanding Officer seized on the possibility of training his bulldozer operators on the development of the cricket pitches in the manner described by the Headmaster. A short time later, a dozen or more bulldozers were busy shifting the soil from the top pitch over the middle pitch and spreading it on the lower pitch. This went on for several days and before long the state of all three pitches was a right mess of soil, stones and boulders.

On the eve of Operation Overlord, the invasion of Europe, the US military in Fermanagh disappeared over-night, including the 'army' of bulldozers. Our cricket pitches remained a sorry mess for many weeks thereafter until a contractor was employed to finish the job.

On Sunday afternoons, we were sent walking into the countryside around Enniskillen. During one such walk, many of us came upon a Flying Fortress aeroplane which had flown from the USA and failed to make it to Killideas airstrip. It was a crumpled mess, containing a lot of attractive objects of interest to us school boys. The guns were still wrapped in brown paper, and there was a great quantity of ammunition in the wreckage. A host of other items, including maps and aeronautical charts, found their way back to the lockers at school. Within few days, we were assembled in the Steel Hall and advised that following the discovery of hazardous things brought into the school, there would be an inspection of lockers.

In the midst of normal school routine, we were aware of the war from the newspapers as well as from the map in the history classroom. Mr Butler ('The Man') showed us the line of each major front, revising daily. But more significantly, in announcements during morning prayers, we were made aware of those boys who had been killed in action. Prefects and Heads of Houses had known these students as seniors, and their reactions to these reports certainly focussed our young minds on the war. I suppose most of us recognised in a strange sort of way that we would take our places in the armed forces if hostilities continued.

With that in mind, and having failed the matriculation, I became aware of openings in the Indian Army, into which two or three of my senior classmates had been recruited on a voluntary basis. I asked to see the Headmaster and duly presented myself to say that I wished to enter the Indian Army. His response was succinct. "Crawford, come back and see me when you have something sensible to talk about." I was in there no more than a minute. A number of attempts to get my wishes across followed, including mention of the fact that my Uncle Eric Macgregor (Gee's husband) was a senior officer, late Commanding Officer, 1st/12th Frontier Force Regiment and currently Commander 20th Indian Infantry Brigade, I failed to convince the man that my mind was made up. The rebuttal simply charged my determination.

About this time, Ian Stewart resigned as Headmaster and went off to the USA as Director of Student Guidance at the University of Pennsylvania. I just hoped that the students there enjoyed more guidance than had been my lot! He was succeeded by the Reverend Douglas Graham, who arrived in naval uniform. He subsequently wore a black cassock, neck to toe, and became known as the Black Abbot. By and by, I decided to make another dive for the Indian Army and arrived in his study for an entirely different experience. For a start, I felt welcome. The proposal was actually discussed and the response positively supportive. Imagine my sheer delight at the prospect of a career in India.

Some weeks later the application forms arrived, one of them dealing with medical aspects. We went through the questions, line by line, until reaching 'Hearing'. Being deaf in one ear, I hesitated. Looking me straight in the face, he said "Yes, indeed you are but you can hear perfectly well in the other one". The answer 'Normal' was ticked and we went on to the next question. Who was I to argue with a naval chaplain?

The application went forward, and in due course I received a letter of acceptance, starting "Dear Sir" and ending "Your obedient servant", with signature followed by "Major General"! At the age of 18, this type of formal signature from a high-ranking officer puzzled me. As the acceptance process continued, I received additional letters similarly signed but never got to meet the Major General.

By the end of my final term in July, 1946, and following several interviews, I was committed for training as an Officer Cadet, Indian Army, at the Brigade of Guards Depot, Caterham, Surrey, starting in the following September. Uncle Eric was pleased to hear of this development and, it was agreed, the best place for me would be the 1st/12th Frontier Force Regiment. I was over the moon with excitement at the prospect of going to India and of the probability of serving in his regiment. On his retirement, he sent me a telegram that read simply "One in, one out. Good luck – Uncle Eric".

– 3 –
The War Years

In 1937, at aged nine, I recall some of the chat about a war in the making. Chat which concerned families in different ways. There were those who avoided mention of it for fear of the consequences and the implications for their businesses and personal well-being, and others who saw the deteriorating situation as one deserving preparation, come what may.

Pa Crawford belonged to the latter category and as if to demonstrate his point of view, he enlisted in the Territorial Army with a commission in the rank of Lieutenant, to serve with the 9th Battery of the 3rd Searchlight Regiment, Royal Artillery. Although the aims and objectives of the TA at the time were all too serious, there was a lighter side in the sense that it was a bit of a club with members from all walks of life joining forces in an attitude of loyalty for the defence of the realm, if need be. Smart uniform appeared and he would frequently be away enjoying himself at the club!

As time passed into 1938, matters in Germany were coming to a head and war seemed inevitable. The lighter side of TA activity turned to training and

My father, second left, with University OTC.

longer spells of absence, for instance at camps. At 11.15 am on the third of September, 1939, the whole nation gathered anxiously around wireless sets and heard Prime Minister Neville Chamberlain: "This morning, the British Ambassador in Berlin handed the German government a final note, stating that unless the British government heard from them by 11 o'clock that they were prepared at once to withdraw their troops from Poland, a state of war would exist between us. I have to tell you now that no such undertaking has been received, and that consequently this country is at war with Germany".

It was pouring with rain as we stood in the drawing room at Arigna, Balmoral Avenue, and digested the momentous significance of the announcement. I remember it well, but was too young to appreciate the implications and the consequences.

Not long after that news the local school, was asked to send senior pupils to the Queen's Hall (Exhibition Centre) to assist with the assembly of gas masks. We collected the various parts of the mask from trays and were shown what to do. The finished job was then inspected by an official before placing the gas mask in a cardboard box with shoulder strap ready for issue. Soon afterwards, everyone was seen going to work, to school or whatever, complete with gas mask.

Some weeks later, Pa went off to camp and the next we heard from him came from France, where the British Expeditionary Force (BEF) of four infantry divisions (150,000 men) had arrived to prepare for the threat of a German attack westward. On 26 May, 1940, the Germans having invaded France and the French having capitulated, the evacuation of the BEF from Dunkirk started. Pa Crawford was a good swimmer and just as well. He entered the water off the beach wearing both suits of service dress uniform, which was all he had left, and swam out to one of the multitude of ships that had arrived to rescue the hundreds waiting. It was a Royal Navy destroyer. Once filled to capacity and beyond, it set off across the channel. Half way across, the ship was hailed by a cruiser and ordered back to the beaches because it appeared from the deck space that there was room for more bodies! Pa's impression at the time was 'Well, this is it'. Back they went, collected more soldiers from the queues extending to chest deep water and made for home a second time. We knew little of the goings on at Dunkirk until hearing that he was safely on terra firma somewhere in the south of England.

There followed a period of uncertainty during which the possibility of an invasion of England seemed imminent. I am not sure how it came about but I became a Messenger in the local ARP (Air Raid Precautions) organisation. I was given a black tin-hat bearing the letters ARP in white and felt very important. Another bit of kit was a rather special gas mask: nothing like as flimsy as those issued to the general public. When the air raid siren sounded a warning, I would cycle off to the local ARP office ready to deal with messages. On one occasion, my attention to duty entailed absence from school. The next day, when I did turn up, my reason for absence was unacceptable. But that was understandable I suppose since Friends School Lisburn was a Quaker establishment and Quakers are pacifists.

At this time, there was much disorganisation, with men of many units all over the place being sheltered, fed, and cared for. It was some time before the survivors could be regrouped, and during this period a change of cap badge took place, namely from Royal Artillery to Royal Engineers.

Apparently, Brigadier Bob McCreary, who had headed Belfast City Transport before the war started and under whom Pa was Permanent Way Engineer, contrived to get Pa transferred to the Transportation Department of the Royal Engineers. The result of this change meant that Pa found himself at Longmoor, which was then the headquarters of the Transportation Service RE, as an instructor in railway engineering and in the rank of Captain. There he remained until November, 1942, when forces were assembled for the First Army's invasion of North Africa (Morocco and Algeria).

Aware that Pa would shortly be leaving the country, destination unknown, Ma decided to slip over to England to bid him farewell. She had a problem, however. He had left Longmoor and she didn't know where he was. In her inimitable way, she boarded the Heysham boat determined to find him, starting at Liverpool. On disembarking at Heysham, she had lost her ticket. The Purser on the Heysham boat wrote on a sheet of paper words to the effect that the bearer, Mrs Crawford, had mislaid her ticket but had paid her fare and was entitled to travel to Bristol via Liverpool. Clutching her piece of paper she set off. It is hard to imagine how she intended to find Pa, who could have been on his way through any number of ports. Having failed to find his unit in Liverpool, she set off for Bristol via London (Euston and Paddington), armed with her piece of paper.

On reaching the gate at Paddington, the piece of paper failed to impress the man on the gate. The train to Bristol was about to leave. In exasperation, she apparently demanded to see the Station Master. An official arrived. She quickly related her association with the Great Northern Railway (Ireland) and her father's position in it before telling the man that her father could tell him a few things about running a railway. She then flourished her piece of paper in his face, ran through the gate, and boarded the train that moved off almost immediately. This tale was subsequently told to me by George Palmer, then in Bristol. Susan Palmer remembered it well.

An armada of 500 ships headed for North Africa carried 107,000 men and thousands of tonnes of weapons and supplies. Included was the 161st Railway Construction Regiment in which Pa, now a Major, was to put his professional railway engineering skills to work. The narrow-gauge coastal railway was old and totally inadequate for carrying tanks. Apart from that, the Vichy French, who opposed the landings, had rendered sections of it beyond repair. The reconstruction of this tenuous means of supply was vital.

At a place named Mateer, in Tunisia, the railway passed through a tunnel that had been mined by the withdrawing enemy force. The mines were evil

THE WAR YEARS

My father with members of his unit in Tunisia.

things called 'S' mines, comprising a small canister of explosive mixed with ball bearings and topped with a stem of three prongs which if depressed caused the canister to explode showering the immediate area with nasty sharp edged bits of metal. A large number of these mines had been embedded in the ballast between the sleepers of the track within the tunnel.

Father went into that tunnel alone on a hand-operated trolley. He carefully disarmed the mines and loaded them onto his trolley, all bar one, which exploded causing a fair amount of damage to his legs as the ball bearings ricocheted around the walls of the tunnel. Long afterwards and at home he showed me remnants of the bearings under the skin. He reckoned he had removed some 90 mines before the explosion. His action on that occasion won him a Military Cross for gallantry and gallant it surely was. He was puzzled on learning from home that he had been awarded the MC because until then he had not been aware of it.

I recall Ma asking me to make a parcel of some things to send to Pa, and to post it at the post office.

Blown Up By Mine, He Carried On

MAJOR Henry Gerald Crawford, Royal Engineers, of Dunmurry, County Antrim, who, as told in yesterday's "Daily Mail," has been awarded the M.C. He was responsible for repairing the important railway to Mateur in April during the advance in Tunisia. He and his unit, without mine detectors, removed 90 enemy mines by primitive methods in 24 hours, and in spite of being "blown up," continued his work of supervising repairs to the railway.

My father awarded the Military Cross.

Unable to find string, I used a handy length of electric flex. In reply, Pa remarked in a letter that the effect of hostilities at home must be pretty serious, i.e. the absence of string. He sent us a box of a dozen lemons. On arrival, just one lemon was rolling around in the box! Lemons being an attractive item in the UK during the war, we were not surprised.

Anxious to do something useful by way of supporting the war effort, Ma joined up as a Censor. This entailed reading mail coming into the country from service men overseas and purging any sensitive detail in the text with an indelible blue pencil. The letters she read and what was written in them completed her education in no uncertain manner, so she said. She made several new friends during her time as a Censor, keeping up with some of them for a long time after the cessation of hostilities.

She also enjoyed voluntary work while assisting with the provision of refreshments at a US Army Club. Frequently, she recalled the significant difference in quality between the social environment enjoyed by the Americans compared with our own service people: the provision of food was a major factor with no thought of rationing. From time to time, she returned home with treats which we assumed were given to the volunteers by way of thanks for their efforts.

On reaching Bizerta via Bone some months later, Pa's men had run out of soap. Being unable to wash oneself properly in a climate of heat and humidity was exceedingly disagreeable. So, he made a trip to the docks where he knew the aircraft carrier HMS *Victorious* was berthed. On approaching the Officer of the Day on board the carrier, he asked if he might have some soap. The officer noting Pa's accent remarked that a colleague on board must also be from the North of Ireland. A few minutes later, Lieutenant Commander Noel Hunter arrived and organised soap, tinned provisions, and other goodies which Pa was pleased to take back with him.

At this time, we at home had moved from Balmoral Avenue to number two Rosemount Terrace, Dunmurry, for fear of air raids on the city. Noel Hunter's father and mother were our neighbours in number three.

Incidentally, Pa established a close relationship with a Tunisian railway engineer in Bone, a man with whom he corresponded in French during several years after the war.

The First Army and the Eighth Army having crushed the Germans and the Italians in North Africa, Mr Churchill set his sights on Italy. Following the invasion of Sicily, the US Fifth Army launched operation 'Avalanche' from North Africa towards Salerno on the east coast of Italy in 1943. As darkness closed in on the evening of 8 September, the 450 ships carrying 69,000 men and 20,000 vehicles approached land with doused lights and took up position in the Gulf of Salerno. Parties of men scrambled down nets into landing craft which moved away to join the other craft circling 4 miles off shore. At 3.30 am, the invaders began landing. On reaching the shore, the landing craft in which Pa found himself, couldn't beach, such was the number of craft already on the shoreline.

The state of the railway on the west coast of Italy had to be seen to be believed. It was chaotic. Long stretches of the track had been bombed, causing the lines to become twisted masses of metal. In other places, the Germans had torn up the track, making the job of reconstruction a nightmare. Before anything could be done by way of restoring the railway, the colossal amount of debris had to be removed. This work went on week after week, and gradually the railway was reconstructed as a means of transporting vital stores towards Naples and beyond.

North of Naples, the railway over the River Volturno had been demolished like everything else. In order to assess the work required and the materials needed to restore the crossing, Pa joined with a group of Italian partisans, presumably familiar with the area. He walked to a position from where the situation could be assessed and then walked along the railway track to a point overlooking the demolished bridge. The partisans slipped away. Although no enemy appeared to be in the immediate vicinity, a fair amount of shrapnel was flying about from the sporadic artillery fire of the withdrawing enemy force.

Demolished bridge, River Volturno, Italy.

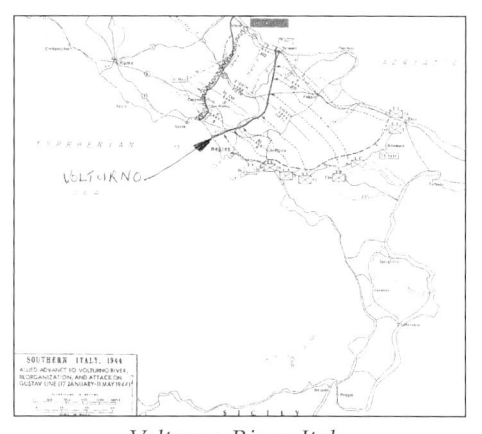

It was never known exactly what hit Father, but he suffered a serious wound to his left chest and could hear air coming in and out. Realising that this was not a good thing, he stuffed a cap comforter/scarf in the wound and stopped the outward flow of air. Losing blood at an alarming rate, he lay down between the rails, wedging his shoulder in an attempt to stop the bleeding. He prepared to die. He didn't expect that the partisans would ever come back, but they did and found him in a bad shape. They carried him back to a medical post, thence down the line to Naples and on a hospital ship bound for Malta, where he was nursed by a quite fearsome naval nursing sister. Shortly after that, Ma heard that his war was over, i.e. on receiving the dreaded OHMS envelope.

Volturno River, Italy.

The demolished bridge was re-built by his regiment but, of course Father never saw the finished job.

In Malta, he hovered between life and death, his chest wound steadfastly refusing to heal. He couldn't take solid food. The only thing he could keep

The new bridge.   *End of the new bridge.*

down was champagne, on which he survived for some four weeks. He subsequently recommended that treatment to all and sundry. My brother-in-law (Consultant) Basil used it many times in his own practice for those in extremis.

Eventually, he returned home from Malta, with his wound still unhealed, and he ended up in Campbell College, Belfast. The school had been taken over as a military hospital, and pupils had been moved to the Northern Counties Hotel, Portrush, Basil included.

In common with established medical thinking at the time, the failure of the wound to heal was attributed to some source of infection – probably dental. As a result, all his perfectly good teeth were extracted. When that failed, it became evident that the chest wound had become tuberculous, probably from reactivation of a healed tuberculous focus which 90%+ of all Irish and Scots (Basil and myself included) carried in their chests.

He was admitted to the Tornadee Sanatorium near Aberdeen, where he underwent several operations under local anaesthetic for the removal of ribs to

Sister Duncan and Dr Kier with my father at Tornadee.

THE WAR YEARS

collapse part of his lung. The infection spread to his spine, causing him to spend eighteen months immobilised in a plaster bed. That he survived, he attributed to a Dr Kier and Sister Duncan, typically never mentioning his own indomitable spirit. The new drug Streptomycin and other agents became available at that time, facilitating in his recovery and return to Belfast to his pre-war work.

There followed a courageous attempt to return to normality, to his job as Deputy General Manager of Belfast City Transport and to the business of reshaping his broken life. The effects of his wound, and I suppose his experiences, the majority of which he kept to himself, gradually took their toll and made it necessary for him to return to hospital at Musgrove Park, where part of his left lung was removed.

I was at school in Enniskillen at the time the bad news was received. Ma thoughtfully decided to go there and tell me about it rather than have me hear by phone. Eileen Semple came with her. Through Uncle Ernie, the Headmaster, Ian Stewart arranged for the newspapers to be withdrawn from the school library on the day the notice about Pa's situation was published. Ian Stewart subsequently made an announcement during prayers in the Steele Hall relating also to the award of the American Bronze Star. The whole action on the west side of Italy was a 5th US Army offensive while the British 8th Army and other allied forces moved up the east side. In recognition of what Pa had done, and before he was moved from the Naples area, a General Gray, US Army awarded him the American Bronze Star in recognition of his gallantry. Their Bronze Star is the equivalent of the British Military Cross, and it is worthy of note that both awards reflected Pa's determination to spare others the risk of injury. In the tunnel at Mateer, he did the job himself, likewise on the Volturno River.

My father awarded the US Bronze Star.

It was at Tornadee that I first appreciated all he had lost from his life on account of the war. I had then joined the Indian Army, and on two occasions I travelled from the Guards Depot at Caterham, Surrey to Aberdeen to spend a while with him. They were not happy times. All around were other men with hideous wounds from service at sea, on land, and in the air. But it was a wonderful hospital where he made, and sadly lost, many friends.

On the conclusion of hostilities we all went to London for the investiture at Buckingham Palace accompanied by Arthur and Eileen Semple. Arthur had been honoured with the MBE. Ma decided to give Sheila and me the opportunity to watch the ceremony and the investment by King George VI, while she

My father on the right following the investiture at Buckingham Palace.

chatted up the policemen at the palace gates. Only two members of the family were allowed this privilege. Ma reckoned we would remember it longer and she was right.

One must remember that in these few pages I have recalled to the best of my knowledge just a few of the incidents and activities about which Pa told me. Brother-in-Law Basil Gray, being at home after I had joined the Army, learnt a good deal more about the incident on the Volturno River and has helpfully related the medical aspects about which I have been unaware. Everything else that happened in all of the weeks, months, and the years of his service from 1937 until 1943, is left to our imagination. One aspect that has always made me happy is that from 'Dunkirk' to the end in Italy, he was doing what he loved and what he was good at, namely building railways. In that respect, he must always have been grateful to Bob McCreary for his initiative in getting him transferred from the Gunners to the Sappers.

Father came home from Malta, invalided out and demobbed, in 1944. I was sent to meet him at Larne. Why Ma didn't come with me I shall never know? I recognised him but his appearance was very different compared with the time, three years previously, when I had last seen him. He remarked afterwards that had he not recognised me, which of course he did, but he recognised his sports coat, his grey flannel trousers and his shoes!

Ma, of course, looked after him hand, foot, and finger. Basil still recalls seeing his breakfast at Arigna – porridge with cream and a raw egg, which he swallowed from a glass, not a pretty sight first thing in the morning.

Following his retirement around 1966, he was able to get about and enjoyed visits to Sheila and Basil then in Kirkcaldy, Fifeshire, and ourselves then in

Edinburgh. He followed the progress of his eldest grandson, Bill Gray, with intense interest and had the pleasure of going to Cabin Hill School to watch him playing rugby. Typically, on that occasion, he remarked "His tackling could stand some improvement!" Pa and Ma paid us a visit in Washington D.C., in 1970, taking the opportunity of a flight chartered by the Irish Rugby team. More about that visit comes later.

On a day in 1972, his health deteriorated rapidly, so much so that Ma phoned me, then in Washington D.C., to say she had arranged with the local Military authority for me to be called home. On arrival in my office the following morning, I found an airline ticket on my desk, with instructions from the Embassy and flew out same evening. Pa was surprised when I arrived at Arigna. I explained that I had been called to an MOD conference at short notice. He smiled, saying "Funny joke, tell me another one." But his indomitable willpower came through once again, and although confined to bed, he survived for a few more years.

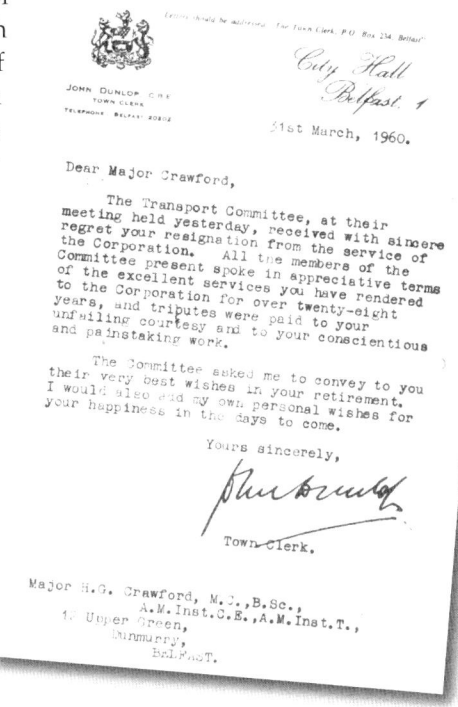

My father resigns from Belfast Corporation due to ill health.

On the occasion of his funeral the Reverend Herbert Irvine found words which seem to me to encapsulate all that Pa was:

> "The presence of such a representative congregation is not only an expression of friendship and sympathy, but also evidence of the esteem in which Major Crawford was held in business, in education, in sport and in church life. In spite of honours won by his own prowess and ability, and honours conferred upon him, he was never tempted to think of himself more highly than he ought. He was a big man in every way. His humility was never a pose; flattery was wasted on him. He was distinguished not only in what he did, but even more in what he was. He served the City of Belfast as Deputy Manager of the Transport Service; he graduated with honours in Queen's University, and was honoured by being elected a governor of Methodist College, Belfast. Major Crawford served with distinction in the 1939-45 war, and for bravery was awarded the Military Cross and the United States Bronze Star Medal. He was

seriously wounded while serving in Italy and for the rest of his life suffered much pain. But he was never one to complain. Deprived of the fullness of physical strength, he had an abundance of moral and spiritual strength which conveyed itself to others and made life easier for them.".

<u>C O L L E G I A N S   C H R O N I C L E.</u>

Vol.1 No.7.   May, 1974.

<u>GERRY CRAWFORD.</u>

On 24th April, Gerry Crawford died. This is a bald statement of fact but within it, there lies a richness of a life of character and quality, and, in relation to Collegians, a remembrance of deep-seated loyalty and interest which for many years served and will continue to serve as a standard for the Club to follow.

Gerry captained the Club in 1927/28 and subsequently was elected President of both Rugby and Cricket Clubs as well as occupying the Chair of the Collegians Club in 1961. He represented the Rugby Club on the Ulster Branch Committee and attained the office of Senior Vice-President of the Branch, but was prevented by ill-health from occupying the Presidency. The Branch presented him with an inscribed plaque on his retirement in recognition of his office and service – the only one of its kind in existence – and just before his death, he handed this over to the Club to be placed alongside other plaques in the Clubhouse. He was appointed a Governor of M.C.B. in 1965 and little brought him greater pride and pleasure than this, for he was a true advocate of "all things Methody", the physical being and image of which he regarded as precious.

It is true to say that a recital of the offices he held do not reveal the real nature of the man. He never took easily to people who made criticism the criterion of comment. He had the respect of all he met. He was sincere, quiet and at times serious, with a naturally bent dry humour. He served in the Forces during the last War with distinction and suffered severe wounds which hampered his movement to a very substantial degree. But such was his determination and courage, he never allowed the illness he subsequently had to endure to daunt his spirit. During the lengthy period he was confined to the house, he enjoyed nothing better than a chat about the Club with his Collegians who came to visit him.

It is difficult to assess what was his most valuable contribution to Collegians because his interest in every aspect of the Club was all-consuming. He was probably at his best in discussion at general committee meetings of the Rugby Club. It was here his real interest lay, and many were the times his wise counsel and straight-forward thinking directed the committee to proper and correct conclusions. By his death, Collegians have lost their oldest stalwart. His influence will undoubtedly continue.

<u>BILL LAVERY.</u>

Tribute to my father from Collegian's Rugby Football Club.

Before closing this chapter, I must mention a few associations from the war years. Arthur Semple, at the Intelligence Branch, Headquarters Northern Ireland District, (NID) was introduced to Ma by somebody or other and subsequently came to live at Rosemount Terrace with his wife, Eileen, and their daughter, Joyce. Prior to that, Arthur had been a regular visitor. On one occasion, he brought with him an elegant young English Intelligence Officer who became another regular visitor with his wife – namely, Michael Dennison and Dulcie Gray — who became well known actors. When performing in one of Noel Coward's plays in London in the early sixties, when Ma and Pa were visiting Sheila and Basil in Harrow, they all went to see the play and afterwards went backstage to renew the acquaintance. On that occasion Pa delivered his famous judgement on English bar measures of whisky – "Away up and get me another of those samples".

Another chap we came to know well was Jimmy Shaw, owner of a smart garage business in Belfast and then Commander, Royal Electrical and Mechanical Engineers, NID. I never met his family but he was very keen on Nora Clarke one of Ma's best friends, taking her on various jaunts including racing in England – there and back by air in one day!

Lastly, Billy Morrow, a divorcé and commercial traveler for Castrol Oils. It would be fair to say that Billy Morrow filled the family gap in Pa's absence during the war.

Ma relied on him a good deal, and they were undoubtedly very close friends. As a regular visitor to our home, the friendship seemed to me to develop into something I found unwelcome. For instance, Billy Morrow's son, Brian, was at school in Coleraine. I was encouraged by his father to visit him although I wasn't very interested. On another occasion, my mother and I travelled to Stranraer, where Father was in charge of the development of the Port of Cairnryan. The port was being constructed by the Royal Engineers for the reception of ships from the USA carrying vehicles and munitions, in preparation for the invasion of Europe. Brian joined us on this trip. A third matter which I found most disagreeable was being ticked off by Billy Morrow for something I had said or done. To use a present-day phrase 'this crossed a red

Supervising the construction of the terminal at Cairn Ryan, Larne, Scotland.

line', and suggested to me that Mr Morrow was establishing himself in a manner which I considered unacceptable. To be blunt, I felt he was behaving like a father figure.

On other occasions we were taken to Bangor for days out and to Portstewart for short holidays. For all of these reasons, I concluded that Billy Morrow's generosity and attention was seeming to prepare for possibility that my father might fail to survive the war. I never thought the relationship with my mother amounted to an 'affair' in the usual sense of the word; none of the illicit thrill of such a thing being secret. Undoubtedly, my mother was lonely. It was as if they'd each found someone necessary, someone who filled an aching gap and made sense of life. Billy Morrow's death from a massive heart attack in 1944 was fortuitous as far as I was concerned.

All of those people were well known to Pa, and on the few occasions when he managed a few days leave, there were memorable parties at Rosemount after which Sheila and I were dispatched to the kitchen to wash dishes into the night.

– 4 –
Joining the Indian Army
1946

Thousands have left Ireland to pursue careers of infinite variety and I imagine most of them felt a twinge of nervousness, if not utter terror, on leaving the security of home. My feelings fell somewhere betwixt the two on boarding the Liverpool boat, but there was an element of excitement that carried me along. It was to be a long journey or so it seemed.

The boat reached Liverpool in the early hours, and the train journey to Euston seemed to take forever. Arriving in the late evening on a cold, wet and gloomy day the appearance of the station did nothing to dispel a niggling feeling that the decision to join the Indian Army might have been foolhardy. But there I was sitting on a seat and collecting my thoughts in the gloomy Euston Station, while clutching my small case of belongings and searching for confidence to complete the trip.

The instructions were to report to the Marylebone Assembly Centre, which was an enormous hotel requisitioned as a transit centre for all kinds of service personnel comings and goings. My room had a bed, a chair, and a table. Nothing else, no carpet, no curtains. Next morning, on joining the queue for breakfast, a Cook Corporal dispensed liver by thrusting his hairy arm up to the elbow into a large tub while fishing pieces of meat from the gravy. A tray of inch thick slices of bread, another with a slab of butter, and a much used tin of marmalade, plus a chipped enamel mug of tea completed my introduction to an Army breakfast.

I escaped from the unpleasantness of the place as quickly as possible, taking the underground to Charing Cross Station and hence to Caterham Station in Surrey, arriving at the time appointed for the rendezvous with the rest of the intake.

About thirty of us found ourselves in the charge of an aggressive NCO who encouraged us into a truck with vigorous wavings of his cane. By and by we arrived at the gates of the barracks, debussed (so he said) and were marched off to Cambridge Block which was to be our abode for the next eighteen months. On the way the sight of five soldiers manacled to each other and running behind an NCO, on a bicycle, to which the leading soldier was attached didn't auger well for the immediate future.

Without a pause we were introduced to two trestles supporting three planks of timber called a bed, three square biscuits called a mattress, a cylindrical thing stuffed with straw called a pillow and four blankets. The NCO then demonstrated the assembly of the bed and the manner in which it was to be made up daily before breakfast parade. Following a chat about what we would be doing on the 'morrow, we made each other's acquaintance. We were all sorts; the tall, the short, the fat, and the thin.

The next port of call was the Barbers' Shop where a team of highly unqualified barbers set to with electric clippers for the short top and sides touch. Next was the Quartermaster's Stores for the issue of battledress uniform, two of, ammunition boots, two pairs, a webbing belt, webbing gaiters, socks, shirts, underwear, towels, a hat, cap badge, housewife (needles and cotton), knife, fork, spoon, mug and a kit bag into which the whole issue was stuffed and signed for. Back in the barrack room we changed into our new clothes and packed what we had brought in a cardboard box. We then went for a meal and, I must say, it was an improvement compared with the London Assembly Centre experience. 'Lights out' to a bugle call meant no light. We floundered about in the dark and collapsed into bed.

'Reveille' to another bugle call came all too soon at 6 a.m. It was dark, cold, and raining outside. We were 'doubled' off to breakfast and after that felt that we could face the day, come what may.

The routine in the Brigade of Guards quickly became clear. All notion of self-esteem, self-confidence, self-opinion, and self-importance was reduced to zero. During this period, there follows a gradual rebuilding of 'self' into a guardsman. This takes quite a long time during which one is subjected to all manner of deprivation and insult. But, in retrospect, it's a good system and it works. One emerges from it a very ordered and organised person with an acute sense of respect for superiors and a huge sense of loyalty to one's fellows. With these attributes confidence and purpose returns and a feeling of pride at belonging to the grand order of things military becomes paramount. There is no doubt that the lessons I learnt about life while at Caterham remain with me to this day. I have not mentioned the word 'discipline' and that is what it was all about. Nothing, not anything was questioned at Caterham. You did it, what ever it was.

One evening a huge US Army vehicle was found parked outside our Cambridge Block. Two of us decided it would hardly remain long in the barracks and would eventually leave. As we had not been out of the place for twelve weeks, here was the chance!

We nipped over the tailboard, lay against it, and waited. Sure enough the engine eventually started and off we went to the main gate, or so we hoped. At the gate we heard the Sergeant of the Guard checking the driver and the clip of his boots as he came round the back to check the interior which, of course, he found empty. We barely breathed as the engine burst into life and the vehicle moved out and into Caterham High Street.

As the first set of traffic lights went red we slipped out and were free! After a few beers and a long chat about our respective pasts, we made our way back on foot. At that hour we were not returning alone and were able to mix up with

JOINING THE INDIAN ARMY

those who had been out legitimately. There was quite a crowd at the guard house door and, we noticed, they were signing in against their names in a massive book, signing on the line on which they had signed out. Well, as we had not signed out, there was only one thing to do, namely disappear when no one seemed to be looking! This we did, but it was a near miss with terrible consequences had we been spotted.

Some weeks later, when 'going out' for Officer Cadets was permitted, a few of us donned our plain clothes, mufti so called, and made our way to the gate, marching of course. The Sergeant of the Guard watched our approach and we wondered what misfortune would befall us – there was always something wrong when cadets attempted to go out. In my case, the ends of my tie were not level. Another cadet was asked to remove his shoe laces, which were found to be a slightly different length, and so on until all of us were sent back to Cambridge Block to correct our faults.

On returning to the gate we got a 'that's better' and having signed out made our way to the bus stop just outside with the Sergeant repeating 'Left, right, left, right ...' A double-decker bus was at the stop. We boarded it and progressing up it's steps, we were still marching with the Sergeant watching us and continuing with his 'Left, right, left' routine. Any faltering and he would have had us off the bus.

My feet did not take kindly to the wearing of ammunition boots and a bone in my right ankle grew like a tomato to such an extent that wearing a boot with the leather laces tied tight was jolly painful. One morning, the Drill Sergeant, noticing that the lace was slack, ordered me to tie it tight which I could not do. "There's nowt wrong with the boot" he said "Its your b...... foot that's the trouble. Report to the MI Room at the double and get them to cut a bit off it. Then report back to me". Ten weeks later I returned from the military hospital at Horley after a minor operation on my foot. On parade next morning, the same Drill Sergeant looked me up and down, "Well Mr Crawford, sir, did you get a bit cut off your foot like I told you?" "Yes, sir," said I. "Good, said he," and that was the end of the story!

I had enjoyed a ten-week break in a surgical ward, playing chess with my neighbour and having a splendid time in all ways. The place was run by QAs, the majority gorgeous girls but the Matron was a witch of a creature. When she arrived every morning, the ward was called to attention. We lay in bed like stiffs, looking directly at the ceiling until she had completed her round.

There was a great maxim for soldiers in training at that time and it was especially applicable at Caterham. It ran "If it moves salute it – if it doesn't, paint it white". Conservancy was the order of each and every day, but once a week it was carried to extremes. We polished the floor of our barrack room until it shone and reflected everything like glass. The edges all round had a nice white line that had to glow. Window panes presented another chore and were cleaned on the outside by standing on the window ledge of the first storey. I recall doing this one day when the Depot Commander strolled by below resplendent in riding boots, British Warm and immaculately turned out. It was bad enough being out there on the window sill and worse when called to attention with both hands and rag tight to one's side. We wrapped bits of blanket around our shoes while polishing for fear of spoiling the areas completed. Blankets were folded in perfect squares with the last blanket wrapped around the others and cardboard inserted in the folds so that the whole was smart and square. On top was laid knife, fork, spoon, razor, hair brush, mug and all in identical order bed after bed. All webbing kit was blancoed in green, brasses polished, boots boned until toe caps shone, and on and on following a weekly routine for CO's inspection. All this was achieved by one helping the other and there, in retrospect, lay another fundamental lesson – inter-dependence upon one's fellows, the old team spirit – it had to be done as a team, there was no other way.

Through this process emerged the natural leaders, those with a bit more character and personality than the rest. We all had some, otherwise we wouldn't have been there, but some had more of it than others. It was interesting to observe this development and it resulted in an informal creation of ranks which subsequently became formal as individuals were recognised, were awarded stripes, and became Cadet NCOs. I managed Lance Corporal, Corporal and Cadet Sergeant by which time life was very much more amenable – i.e. doing the shouting rather than being shouted at!

Drill on the Barrack Square was a daily engagement, and under the supervision of an unspeakably terrifying succession of Drill Sergeants we became pretty good at it. But when we were off colour, so to speak, all hell was let loose. We were doubled round the Square until we nearly dropped with exhaustion. This, I suppose, kept us lean and fit? And every now and again the dreaded call 'Take that Cadet's name' would precede the march to the guard room and a spell on fatigues, e.g. peeling a mountain of potatoes or cleaning metal coal bins until they shone like all else in the place. I made a great job of one such coal bin one evening only to have it placed outside for the night during which time a thin layer of rust came upon it. It had to be done again next day. And if one qualified for a Saturday afternoon's confinement to the Square, there was a bit of drill followed by the cleaning of a square yard or so with a tooth brush while wearing full drill order of dress.

These possibilities sort of encouraged one to steer clear of trouble. Route marches up and down the hills around the town were another frequent occupation. At quieter times, we studied map reading, fired our weapons, and generally learned everything expected of soldiers and would-be officers.

One dark day in 1947, we were assembled for a chat by a visiting senior Indian Army officer from the War Office. In the course of a very short briefing, we were told that due to the problems in India, we would not be going to Officer Training at Bangalore after all.

The disappointment was felt in all sorts of ways. Going off to Bangalore had been the focus of our attention and the reward for our achievements in all of those eighteen months. As our engagement in the Indian Army had been of a temporary nature pending commissioning, we found ourselves free to return to civil life. We were given a few days in which to choose disengagement altogether or transfer to the British Army. Talking about it amongst ourselves helped the process of reaching a decision and an important one at that.

Some had had enough and jumped at the opportunity of getting out. Others, like myself, had gained much from the Caterham experience and, as in my case, felt that to turn it in would be a sort of failure. Besides, what else might I have done? The notion of University, supposing I had the ability to gain a place, did not appeal. Nor did the prospect of some hum-drum occupation like getting a job. So, some days later I, with souls of similar thoughts on the matter, formed up outside one of the offices. We entered, one by one, stood to attention before an Indian Army officer and were discharged with that word rubber stamped across our Army Books 64 (we all had one of those!). A Brigade Sergeant Major then ordered "One pace right close march" and, one by one, we found ourselves before a British Army officer who handed us new ABs 64 and asked us to sign an enlistment form. In that short time, we had left the Indian Army and joined the British Army on a permanent engagement but not as Officer Cadets – just plain private soldiers.

By and by, we were introduced to the possibility of going to Sandhurst and gaining a commission. Meantime, we continued with a bit of drill and were otherwise occupied cleaning things and trying to keep warm in the bitterly cold winter of 1947. It was a sort of phoney existence; no one bothered with us much and the previously fierce routine slipped away. Life was much relaxed. We were really something of a nuisance. It must be remembered that during this post-war period, a majority of officers were looking forward to demobilization and 'civvy street'.

Things looked much brighter when the letters arrived notifying us that we were to appear before a Regular Commissions Board (RCB), the result of which would determine whether or not we would go to Sandhurst. On assembling at the appointed place and time, we each fitted a cloth thing on which was printed a number, back and front in large numerals. This was to be our identification for the next three days. Just about everything we did was observed by a team of officers who marked us continuously on their mill boards. We were marked while eating, while walking about the place, while entering into discussion about various tricky topics (including politics), and most particularly while doing practical tests and when put in charge of the group.

The test I led involved moving a 45-gallon oil drum across a 'minefield' (represented by two white tapes on the ground) using timbers, none of which was quite long enough to span the gap, some cordage, a few pickets, a sledge hammer and, of course, the muscle of the half dozen members of the team. There was no preparation for this exercise and time was limited to fifty or so minutes. There was no space for mistakes. Somehow or other one had to succeed. We tied pairs of the timber spars together with the intention of rolling the drum to the other side but half way the setup sagged under the weight of the drum and the guys balancing on the spars. Back they came under orders, there had to be lots of orders. We tightened the cordage and tried again without success. With time running out, I decided the best solution would be to make an 'A' frame, tie the drum to the top of it, carry the legs to the edge, heave the end with the drum to the sky and lower it to the other side.

With much puffing and groaning, the operation was completed except that we were not across ourselves as was part of the requirement. The lightest lad in my team was 'ordered' across by making his way over the spars. Having released the drum we recovered the 'A' frame, tied a second 'A' frame which was passed across and stood up on the other side. Between the two we fitted the rest of the cordage, tied the ends to a picket driven into the ground on each side and, one by one, made our way across hand over hand. The expressions on the faces of the folk doing the marking did nothing to suggest either success or failure. Discouragement seemed par for the course.

At the end of it all, we gathered in a room for the final chat, for the results, and for departure with the coach waiting outside. A Major General, no less, gave a pep talk to the effect that not all of us had succeeded and that there was no shame about that. As we filed out of the room each member was handed his result with a few paragraphs of comments on an A4 sheet of paper. At the top right hand corner of my sheet I saw the letter 'F', screwed up the paper, stuffed it in my pocket and made for the coach. David Downes, whom I had teamed up with while at Caterham, was following. In his inimitable Welsh accent he said "How did you do boyo?" "Failed" said I as he showed me his form with the letter 'C' in the first paragraph. At the top on the right was an 'F'?? I quickly retrieved my crumpled paper to find 'B' in the first paragraph. On seeing 'Form F' I had read no further!

– 5 –
Sandhurst
1948

The British Army boasted three establishments: The Royal Military Academy Sandhurst, Camberley (RMAS), The Royal College of Science, Shrivenham (RCS), and The Staff College, also at Camberley. In the course of a successful career, an officer might attend all three and certainly two of them – RMAS leading to a commission, RCS and/or Staff College a few years later. Senior rank, e.g. Colonel and above, would not normally be achieved without either RCS or Staff College. It is unlikely that a General officer would not have attended Staff College.

Prior to World War II, Engineers and Gunners went to Woolwich, known as 'The Shop', to become officers while Infantrymen and the Cavalry went to Sandhurst. On the conclusion of hostilities, it was decided to organise all regular officer training at Sandhurst. There were three colleges at Sandhurst, Old College, with four companies named after First World War campaigns, Victory College, with four companies named after Far East campaigns (WW II), and New College, with four companies named after European campaigns (WW I & II).

The first Intake in 1947 (Intake 1) occupied about 50% of the Old College accommodation, with the other two colleges unoccupied. Intake 1 was a vanguard, so to speak, or a means of trying out the routine that would ultimately apply to all three colleges. The intake which I joined was Intake 1A, which completed the complement of Old College and 50% of New College.

I was posted to Blenheim Company. We became known as the 'Bastard Intake'! After six months in Blenheim, it was decided to use Intake 1A to launch Victory College, together with the new Intake 2. I found myself transferred to Burma Company where I remained for the rest of the two-year course.

The initial routine at Sandhurst reflected much of the Caterham experience, more drill under Brigade NCOs and Warrant Officers. Each company had its own Company Sergeant Major (WO 2) and each College its own Regimental Sergeant Major (WO 1), and a number of Sergeants in each company completed the establishment. But there were welcome differences, e.g. we had our own rooms and Mess life was run along the lines of an Officers' Mess. We had general military training in Military History, Accountancy, Map Reading, Military Writing, and in several other such topics there was purely academic training in languages, mathematics and science. So, one might say the programme had similarities to a University routine but with a military dimension. One was conscious throughout the training of being prepared to become an exceptionally well-trained young officer. The standards were high, as was the quality of the training. This was achieved by instructors in all departments of particularly high calibre. Whether officers, NCOs, or Warrant Officers, they had, without exception, been hand-picked for the job and had oodles of experience. It was a great place to be and I enjoyed every moment while there.

An annual occasion was The Sovereign's Parade. We were privileged during my time at Sandhurst to parade before King George VI. It was a quite wonderful experience. Having been on parade in steady rain for an hour or more before His Majesty arrived, we were soaked! And he got pretty wet as well – no rain coat. He inspected all twelve hundred of us from an open Land Rover while Queen Elizabeth and the young princesses watched from the saluting base. Having trooped the Colours and marched past in both slow and quick time, we returned to our respective Company areas, were dismissed to hand in our weapons and proceed immediately to the Victory College Mess for lunch. As it was Victory College's Day, the royal party had lunch in our Mess. The time from marching off the parade ground, until standing behind our chairs in the Mess can't have been more than twenty minutes. The King arrived a few minutes later having changed into an identical dry uniform plus regalia. Quite a feat, I should say.

On another occasion we were paid a visit by Field Marshall Montgomery, who also took luncheon in the Victory College Mess. He left his famous beret on the table in the entrance hall of the College, and following lunch, it was nowhere to be seen? We cadets sat cross-legged on the floor of the gymnasium for his address which he opened with some disappointment over the loss of his beret. He felt improperly dressed. By the end of the programme, his beret had been found hanging over the head of a lion decorating the entrance hall. Inside was found a piece of paper inscribed "The British Lion roars"! I expect he got to hear about this prank and he would not have been amused by it. For those less familiar with his reputation, I should mention that while he was held in high regard by many, there were many more who didn't share that esteem. This division of regard for him had roots in his alleged showmanship before, during, and after the Battle of Alamein and his ruthlessness when sacking unwanted members of his staff, some of them of near contemporary rank.

Every now and again, an evening lecture would be given on some particular aspect of the war by a senior personality. The occasion I shall always remember was the lecture given by Admiral Sir John Tovey, who had been Commander in Chief of the Home Fleet and responsible for the sinking of the *Bismarck* on 27 May, 1941. Supported with slides depicting the changing stations of the ships, projected on a huge screen, it was nothing less than brilliant. The course of that historic naval engagement was followed almost day by day from the departure of the *Bismarck* from the Baltic to the demise of the greatest battleship in the world in the Bay of Biscay. The quality of the accompanying narrative was such that one shared the sense of responsibility, the risks taken, the alternating moments of crisis, success and more crises, and the courage of all those involved, both British and German.

The story of the sinking of the *Bismarck* is worthy of a read by anyone at any time. The day before the sinking, the *Bismarck* had vanished! Various sorties by Swordfish aircraft failed to locate her. The British had lost the scent! Following the breaking of a coded message transmitted from the *Bismarck* a Coastal Command Catalina flying boat knew where to look. The *Bismarck* was located through a chink in the clouds and it's position signalled back to the fleet. That particular Catalina had flown from the Killadeas Base on Lough Erne where those of us in the School Air Training Corps had spent many happy times. We often flew out over the Atlantic in Catalinas and Sunderlands and were usually afforded a spell in the driver's seat which mid-teens was very exciting indeed.

The end of the course at Sandhurst was marked by a ball and a few days later by the Passing Out parade. A great pal of mine knew a couple of lassies at the Holloway Ladies College near Egham. They leapt at the opportunity of accompanying us to the ball. We set off to collect them in good time and had a hilarious time into the early hours. The best of the three orchestras was Edmundo Ross'.

I can't remember the names of the other two, but they were top-drawer at the time. Anyhow, as the evening bore on my friend and I realised that we would not be able to return our ladies to the College and get back in time for Breakfast Roll Call parade (BRC). So, we approached our Company Commander and sought permission, in the circumstances, to be excused BRC. He seemed very amiable to such an extent that we decided it would be in order to miss the parade.

Well, following a distinctly wobbly ride to Egham and back, sections of it on pavements, we rolled up to the Square just as the BRC was being dismissed. The Sergeant Major aware of both our absence and our arrival accosted us with unspeakable fury, summoned a couple of NCOs and placed us in close arrest.

We were incarcerated in the cells below Old College to await our fate. In due course, we were arraigned before the Company Commander on a charge of absence from parade. When invited to explain ourselves the Company Commander heard us out before saying "I have no idea what you are talking about"! or words to that effect. He had forgotten our amiable conversation during the early hours or, shall we say, chose not to remember.

After threats of commissioning being postponed, we were dismissed to live another day. The process of clearing up the grounds and accommodation following the Ball had amusing aspects, e.g. young ladies seeking to get home in broad daylight having lost track of their partners in the rush and not understanding the impetuous attitude of those chasing them off the premises.

Mr Brand was RSM when I arrived at Sandhurst. He had served during both world wars and chose to wear the 1914-1918 style of uniform – knickerbockers, puttees, and a short jacket. In order to co-ordinate the drill movements of one hundred or so cadets on parade, it was customary for us to shout out the time with each movement, i.e. "One, Two and Three". One morning he called the attention of one of the drill sergeants instructing him to call out the time. The sergeant replied "It's arf past ten, Sir." The sergeant, who incidentally held the VC (Victoria Cross for gallantry in action) was immediately arrested and marched off the parade.

That incident was an example of the humour underlying the serious and demanding business of drill parades. On another occasion, having ordered "Right Dress", to achieve three ranks in a dead straight line, the Adjutant (mounted on horse) called out "What's the dressing like Mr Brand?" "It's appalling, Sir," he replied. On each subsequent occasion, when the Adjutant asked the same question we would all whisper "It's appalling, Sir". Although the whispers of a great many cadets was clearly audible, they were ignored.

On the retirement of Mr Brand, who took over The Jolly Farmer pub outside Camberley, J C Lord was appointed RSM. He had been a POW and quite famous having drilled the prisoners at his camp armed with broom sticks. The Brigade of Guards standard achieved made a huge impression on the Germans. He was a tall man, a decisive fellow and highly respected in Army circles. When addressing a new intake of cadets, he was known to say "I shall call you, Sir, and you will call me Sir, the only difference being that you mean it whereas I don't. Jesus Christ is in charge up there (pointing to the sky), I'm in charge down here." On Saturday mornings, the drill parade ended about noon after which we were free for the weekend. Come noon, we could hear the trains leaving Camberley Station while J C Lord deliberately delayed our departure with a pep talk about one or other of his many experiences.

We seldom got away before 12.30, which was exasperating since lots of leisurely arrangements were ruined. For instance, when my friend David Downes invited me to his home in Hereford, we missed our train but caught another that took us as far as Ledbury. We walked the railway track for the remaining 12 miles, arriving in Hereford at 2 a.m.

The Passing Out parade, for which we had prepared for several weeks, was quite something. This was watched by Ma Crawford, and George and Susan Palmer. Commissioning at last with our Commission documents signed by King George VI. Having joined the Indian Army from school in 1946, commissioning into the Corps of Royal Engineers in 1948 marked the end of a period of uncertainty and the start of a proper and secure career. The Sandhurst intake being the first post-war placing in the various regiments was very competitive. We could choose where we wanted to go, but in a majority of cases infantry and cavalry regiments offered few places and those whose applications succeeded had territorial and other advantages, e.g. family connections. I decided to go for the Sappers.

SANDHURST

Harry commissioned from Sandhurst.

– 6 –
School of Military Engineering
Chatham, 1949

Our batch of some 26 Young Officers assembled at Charing Cross Station for the trip to Brompton Barracks, Chatham, where we would be training in the business of military engineering. Once aboard the train, we observed that one of the party in our compartment was wearing pips with a red background, whereas RE pips have a blue background! By the time we reached Chatham Station, the offending things had been feverishly removed and replaced with those from a second uniform in one of the suitcases. What would have happened had he arrived at the SME with red pips, goodness knows.

The YO training course equipped us with similar knowledge compared with that of the sappers (In RE parlance 'Sapper' is the equivalent of 'Soldier'). The training was largely practical in bridging, mine warfare, demolitions, and watermanship. It was hard work but good fun as well. We were introduced to a series of Royal Engineer Supplementary Pocket Books in which could be found the answers to just about any question from the quantity of water consumed by a camel in any twenty-four-hour period to the strength of a baulk of timber of any type and dimension. By the end of the course, we had acquired as much information about sapper tasks as we would need as Troop Commanders and, most importantly, we had done it all!

Mess life at Chatham was great. The mix of senior and junior officers quickly put us right on Corps customs and traditions. For instance, no one, but no one, spoke at breakfast! I learnt that early one morning when sitting down to breakfast in the HQ Mess I said "Good morning" to a Major across the table. He replied, "Good morning, good morning, good morning and may that last you for the rest of your career!" I hid behind my newspaper propped up on one of the wooden stands provided for that purpose. During dinner, which on Guest Nights went on for a very long time, we would open a book for bets (one shilling in a bowl) on the time when the President would rise and conclude the proceedings. By that time, most of us were in dire need of relieving ourselves but one dare not leave the table. The only way out, if need be, was to slip under the table and crawl amongst the feet to the end whereupon the swing doors would mysteriously open and close without a soul in sight. Sometimes the feet of brother officers would strike out at the body below with disastrous and sometimes damp consequences.

After dinner on these special occasions, we all played games of a physically demanding nature. Ten or so YOs would form a circle, arms over shoulders, on top of which would stand another eight or so bodies and so on until one wretched YO had to climb to the top and touch the ceiling. More often than not the pyramid would collapse causing much anguish. If it didn't collapse naturally, cushions hurled at the legs of the lot at the bottom ensured a mangled heap of bodies. 'High Cockleoram' was a favourite involving one team of, say, eight with heads between legs of the chap in front while another team jumped on the backs of the 'snake', with the object of bringing the other team to the floor. And 'Boat Racing' – two teams seated in a row on the floor with the front men holding a broom handle. It was a sort of tug o' war, won by the first team to wrench the broom handle from the opponents. And 'Freda' – that was tremendous fun. It was played around a full size billiard table with just one billiard ball which had to be kept on the move and could be played only from either end of the table. The two teams of contestants did their best to prevent the opposition from playing the ball from table end. Shirts were frequently ripped from bodies and, in the event of the ball leaving the table, there were cuts, bruises, and abrasions galore. These games were played following a good five-course dinner, during which a liberal quantity of wine had been consumed. That, with pints of beer during the proceedings, made for an exceedingly rough house! It was a means of releasing young men's high spirits and it surely toughened them up.

Being deaf in one ear, I found it necessary to have my good ear syringed from time to time. While at Chatham, this was usually done by a nurse at the Royal Navel Hospital. However, on a particular occasion I was received by an RN Surgeon Captain no less. He was the spit and image of James Robertson Justice, with large bushy beard and appropriately large stature. He sat on a three-legged milking stool and examined my ear. Having done the necessary, he asked, "And how did you get into the Royal Engineers with a deaf ear?" The question concerned me a great deal because it might have resulted in my being boarded medically with interference to my career progress. As I withdrew from the situation, he slapped me on the back and exclaimed "Good luck boy!"

For the wet bridging and watermanship parts of the course, we moved to Ripon in Yorkshire. A ball was arranged during our time there, not quite on the scale of the Sandhurst Ball but not far short of it.

We YO's didn't have girlfriends at Ripon; there wasn't time for that and, in any case, we didn't know anyone locally. Nevermind, the powers that be arranged for us to attend a Young Conservatives Ladies Dance at which we would have an opportunity of inviting a partner to the Ball. Off we went in a Troop Carrying Vehicle to the dance in Ripon.

With every girl determined to win an invitation, and with more girls on hand than YO's, it was a highly competitive dance. A fly on the wall would have been amused at the process of twenty five amourous young men assessing the forms of some thirty or more equally amourous young women. I sorted out a partner fairly early and we danced and talked together for the rest of the evening. At the conclusion of the programme, the girls went off to get their coats and returned as we were filing out of the building. I saw my partner whom I had invited, with time and place, and waving to her said, "See you Friday" to which she responded quite positively. Well, she would, wouldn't she!

On the night of the ball, we assembled in the Hall of the Mess awaiting our partners and by and by, they all arrived. While enjoying a few drinks in table parties of twelve or so happy people, the Mess Steward tapped my shoulder and said very quietly, "Mr Crawford, your partner is waiting in the Hall." To make a long story short, the girl I had waved to on leaving the dance was not the one I had spent the evening with – I had invited two girls! Comradeship came to the fore. How my fellow YO's managed to conceal my error of judgement I shall never know but some how or other we got everyone in our party nicely mixed up and had a thoroughly enjoyable time into the early hours. I like to think that my partners were unaware of my bungle but can't be sure about that. Perhaps they knew each other!

– 7 –
No. 1 Training Regiment RE
Malvern, 1949

1 TRRE was based at Merebrook Camp at the foot of the Malvern hills in Worcestershire. It had been a hospital during the war and comprised rows of very ordinary looking red brick buildings, with concrete passageways between. The mortuary was the Armourer's den, complete with tiled slab on which he attended to rifles and machine guns, etc. Our quarters were Nissen huts (tunnel shaped buildings with a bathroom in the middle serving each half in which two of us made a home).

This was my first taste of National Service which was the reason why the sappers were there. They were in parties of thirty or so men, each party in the charge of a YO, a Sergeant, and a couple of Corporals. Some of the YO's were National Servicemen, others, like myself, were regulars. The Quartermaster Sergeant Instructors (QMSIs) were experts in the business of field engineering. As well as discharging our duties as YOs in charge, we were actually continuing our training and learning to be effective Regimental Officers. It was a most useful experience and by the end of it, we had mastered all sorts of unfamiliar procedures, e.g. balancing acquittance roll accounts after Pay parades, taking charge of live firing on the ranges, and supervising the training programme and daily routine for our parties.

The training was quite gruelling for the sappers, so much so, in one instance, that a sapper shot and killed the party Corporal in a fit of aggression in his barrack room. This was, of course, murder and the implications of it sent much alarm through the camp. The Corporal's home was in Belfast and, not surprisingly I suppose, yours truly was given the unenviable task of taking his remains home. It was an awesome job dealing with a coffin in the guards van of the train, not to mention the hold of the Liverpool boat and the reception by wailing relatives on arrival. One did one's best, but it was difficult in the home and at the funeral.

I had a bit of a flair for markmanship, having been a keen participant in 0.22 smallbore shooting at Portora. The Colonel, keen to enter a regimental team at Bisley, sent me off with a dozen other good shots to a local firing range, where we lived for a fortnight shooting 0.303 weapons all of most days. By the end of it, we had all improved our skill and a team for Bisley was selected.

The competitions during the annual Bisley week were open to both service and civilian competitors, and as you can imagine, the standard of markmanship was exceptionally high. I recall a chap next door to me on the range placing his rounds of ammunition in a small bucket of water. He explained that he did this lest it should rain, and that rain would interfere with the accuracy of his shots! Others would lie on their backs with the rifle supported between their feet as a means of greater accuracy. We didn't win anything outright but managed second or third places in a few of the many competitions.

Nowadays, ear defenders are worn but in my day one relied on pieces of cotton wool stuffed into ears. There can be little doubt that concentrated rifle shooting then and subsequently played a part in the deterioration of my hearing. I would come off the ranges with a high pitched whine in my good ear, such that I could hear nothing else for some hours.

For demolition training, we took our parties to local farms in response to the acceptance of the Regiment's offer to demolish hedgerows, create ponds, and other jobs. The sappers were taught safe ways of handling explosives and detonators before applying their skills to various targets. The object of this training was to teach the safe use of explosives and, of course, to eradicate fear of them.

For watermanship, we rowed assault boats, built ferries, and Bailey bridges on the Severn at Upton. This part of the course, though hard work, was enjoyed by all. Another aspect of the course was the sterilization of water pumped from the river into inflatable tanks for the creation of a water point. Although I had learnt how to do all these things during the initial visit to the SME, the opportunity of teaching others and dealing with the inevitable problems that occur consolidated my knowledge.

Harry operating a raft, River Avon, Tewkesbury.

The Dock Strike in 1950 provided a welcome interruption to the repetitive routine at Malvern. Several parties were bussed up to London, accommodated in the Underground tunnel shelters that had been used during the blitz. The shelters were furnished with row upon row of three-tier bunk beds with washing facilities, latrines, and catering provided deep below the city.

Each morning, we assembled on the street before embarking on a convoy of three-ton vehicles escorted by police on motor cycles for the trip to the docks where ships were lying idle and awaiting urgent unloading of cargoes with a good many others waiting beyond in the Thames estuary. There were hundreds of servicemen on the job. It was my first experience of the army dealing with an emergency situation.

I recall two incidents that were amusing at the time but probably anything but amusing as far as the authorities on the docks were concerned. While unloading a cargo of timber from Canada, we noticed that the surface of the timber in the hold had been painted with strips in various colours. Oblivious of the reason for this, we busied ourselves with long handled spikes and wire slings for the shifting of the timber by derricks onto the quay. The priority, encouraged by the ship's officers and crew, was to empty the hold so that the ship could get away. Soft drinks and aluminium buckets of fruit salad came in unlimited quantities! What we didn't know was that the painted timbers at various levels indicated the extent of individual and contracted consignments. Timbers of many sizes and with all sorts of colours painted thereon were stacked neatly on the quay.

Another ship we dealt with had a cargo of sugar amongst other commodities – huge sacks of it. Our sapper crane driver got a bit carried away and accidentally lowered one of the sacks into the Thames. It was retrieved as a sodden stinking mess and half the original size!

The Regiment was host to a party of cadets from a school in Birmingham for a couple of weeks and it fell to me to organise a programme of training. Those young men certainly benefited from a taste of the army proper, especially while under the eagle eye of the Drill Sergeant.

It was during my time at 1TRRE that I experienced my first attempt to defend a sapper on a charge for some offence that escapes my mind. At the conclusion of my defence, I declared that the offended should not be found guilty whereupon the Major, presiding over the matter, picked up a paper-punch and threw it at me saying "It is I, not you, who will decide the matter of guilt!" Lesson learnt!

The CO, when I arrived, was Lt Col Foster. Keen to make provision for watermanship training near to Merebrook Camp instead of 6 miles distant at Upton-on-Severn, he arranged for the creation of an extensive pond in nearby woods. It was known as Foster's Folly since it failed to contain any water. The next CO was Lt Col Holbrook who had a fear of dogs, especially Gus Sinclair's Alsation, and so much so that he carried a golf club when moving between the Mess Lines and the HQ offices! I

Harry's Blue Roan Cocker Spaniel, Betsy.

myself had a blue roan Cocker Spaniel, Betsy, with whom I walked the Malvern Hills on many occasions.

The Adjutant, John Notley, and the Assistant Adjutant, Johnny Fowles kept the Regiment up to speed. Johnny Fowles took me to his home in Cheam one weekend where I met a most attractive young lady who accompanied me a while later to the Mess Dance. A romance developed and I enjoyed many visits to her home in Ealing, where Saturday night parties went on into the early hours followed by Sunday morning gatherings at a local club.

As a match seemed possible, I took her home to Dunmurry, but she proved an expensive lass with expensive ideas, so I allowed the relationship to fizzle out! Her place was taken by a young lady in Hereford introduced by David Downes. Once again, I was made welcome in a home, her home and stayed there on many occasions. She also accompanied me home to Dunmurry, by which time Ma must have been getting a bit tether ended over trips around the North of Ireland one after the other! But that association, also quite promising at the time, fizzled out! It was just as well on both counts as in retrospect I don't think either of them would have been successful Army wives! Pa remarked at the time, "The girls that are fun don't always make the best wives!" Good advice!

I was quite glad to move on from 1 Training Regiment RE where the routine of training National Service intakes was very repetitive. I was anxious to join a unit where there was a job to be done, but before that I had to return to the School of Military Engineering.

– 8 –
School of Military Engineering
Chatham, 1950

Our Sandhurst batch returned to the School for the second phase of YO training – a Supplementary Course to add meat to the bone – technical training and design in various categories, such as the supply of electricity and water to camps, the construction of buildings, the assessment of materials required, and so on. Having learnt the theory, we were sent off in syndicates to design all sorts of schemes. This was interesting work done over several days and sometimes a week or more. Now and again, we would elect one or two members of the syndicate to complete the scheme, while the rest of us shot off for a few days.

During this time, we visited several major civil engineering projects. A section of tunneling for the railway through the Pennines, the construction of a dam in Wales, and the construction of a deep water dock on the Manchester Ship Canal come to mind. These opportunities provided an insight into the planning and execution of very large engineering schemes and the interesting ways in which problems were resolved.

Mess life continued as previously – dinners followed by games and a good deal of drinking! By the end of the course, we had acquired a broad knowledge of everything a Sapper officer might be called upon to do and, most importantly, a knowledge of the many manuals for reference since all of the detail could hardly be remembered.

After the war, the Royal Engineers acquired two 30-square-metre yachts renamed *Avalanche* and *Overlord*. I believe they were part of the post-war reparation programme and were found in Kiel harbour. From time to time, retired officers would sail these boats and enlist crews by phoning the HQ Mess Secretary, who would make enquiries amongst the young officers on training courses. I recall such an occasion when Frank Carus and I volunteered to crew for a retired Major General and his Brigadier friend, who were making preparations at Buckler's Hard on Southampton Water. We set off on Frank's motorbike and after a couple of hours found the seniors shifting supplies of food and booze on board *Avalanche*. It was proposed to make for the Channel Islands next morning.

The weather looked promising, with a fair breeze and good visibility. On reaching the Needles, we encountered a steep swell caused by the incoming tide and the opposing wind. I was on the foredeck while Frank, with more experience, was with the seniors in the cockpit. By and by, the Major General, feeling a bit queasy, decided to retire below. Frank took the helm and a short time later, as the swell became uncomfortable, the Brigadier decided to join his friend below. That left Frank and I to manage the boat, as we headed out from Southampton Water.

All was well until we agreed that we should not attempt to continue towards the Channel Islands. The problem then was how to go-about in such a sea. Some 300 yards to windward, a submarine surfaced: a black and rusty object. A crew member appeared at the top of the conning tower, and using a loud hailer, enquired whether or not we were ok. As we were certainly not OK, we indicated our concern with three thumbs pointing down, the fourth on the hand on the helm! Whereupon the submarine moved slowly round to our windward side, came quite close and provided a comparatively quiet sea. Frank yelled "Lee-Ho" and round we went. We left the submarine behind, with no knowledge of its name or position and headed back to Buckler's Hard!

It was during this time that I met the young lady I should have married. I can't go into details because I would not wish our relationship to be discovered. She was the tops, from an Army family, and went on to be a professional singer. We had great times together, hunting, walking, and visiting her friends. I have always regretted drawing our association to a conclusion for the wrong reason – I just didn't think I was good enough for her. It was a big mistake, and I often think how different the life ahead would have been had I been more sensible.

– 9 –
32 Assault Regiment RE
1951

I felt fortunate to be posted to this particular regiment, which was rather special. It had been part of the 79th Armoured Division for the D-Day landings and beyond into Europe. We had Churchill and Sherman tanks, the former capable of carrying bridge spans, fascines of chestnut palings for the filling of ditches, rotating flails (chains) for the clearance of minefields, ploughs for the destruction of roads, a massive bulldozer blade, and a weapon for the projection of demolition charges that would make a severe dent in almost anything. They were formidable machines.

One of the traditions on joining a regiment was the presentation of visiting cards to encumbent families by new arrivals. In the past, cards would have been received by butlers and servants and presented to the lady of the household on a silver salver. In my day, the card got shoved through the letter box quietly so that the lady of the household would not hear the noise and come running to the door to face a sheepish subaltern with not much to say!

Based at Cambrai Barracks, Perham Down above Tidworth, I was appointed Troop Commander No. 2 Troop of 26 Assault Squadron, with five Churchill tanks. We spent a good deal of time training on Salisbury Plain – lots of exercises with the objective of perfecting the skills involved when operating the devices carried on the vehicles. This had a political objective since the Royal Armoured Corps resented the existence of 'armour' under Royal Engineer cap badges! In order to retain and perpetuate our role, we had to be good at it.

Exercise "Hopalong" was arranged with the objective of testing all of our skills and the movement of the armoured vehicles. The Regiment setting off across Salisbury Plain was a sight well remembered. The route took us north of Amesbury and hence to Salisbury, Blandford, Bere Regis, and on to the Royal Armoured Corps Depot at Lulworth, during the course of three days. At Bere Regis, one of my Churchill tanks became severely bogged down in a swamp. We eventually towed it out using the other four tanks in a 'Y' formation, the towing vehicles joined together with the 100-ton steel wire ropes carried for such situations. At one stage, my tank driver opened the engine hatches to adjust the clutch. This involved removing a few bolts. When returning the bolts he used his finger to find the holes. Just at that moment his National Service co-driver, sitting bored in the driver's seat, just happened to touch the starter button! Many years later, a chap came up to me in the street. "How's things with you, sir?" I didn't recognise him until he held up his hand with the end of one finger missing!

Mess life was great with some twenty subalterns and three majors living on the premises. While at Perham Down, I bought my first car – a 1926 Clyno. I found it in a shed belonging to the Vicar of Abbott's Ann, an adjacent village. It was in a sorry state of appearance, was a non-runner, and had to be towed back to the barracks! But, nevertheless, good value for £25. Needless to say, all of the resources needed to get the car back on the road were available. We had a Royal Electrical and Mechanical Engineer unit attached with not a lot to do!

By and by, the engine was attended to and several coats of British Racing green paint applied. The car then joined the others in the Mess garage, namely an ancient Rolls Royce, a Salmson, two Bentleys, an Alvis and several 'ordinary' saloon vehicles, all of which were frequently seen parked outside the pub at Chute. Compared with the maintenance routine today, I could complete a top-overhaul during a weekend. My only regret was having to part with it on being posted abroad at the end of the tour of duty. It would have been worth a bob or two today.

One evening after a Dinner Night (a fairly formal monthly occasion in full bib and tucker), a few of us strayed down to the Tedworth Club in the Clyno to make a fuss of the ever so lonely QA nurses who were billeted on the top floor. On returning to our Mess where my compatriots debussed, I drove the car into the garage. On arriving at the front door, a most angry Major confronted me saying "Crawford, what on earth do you mean by it?" "Mean about what, Sir?" says I. "There are two QA nurses in the Mess which is forbidden at anytime, let alone on a Dinner Night". I really didn't know that they had been in the car and collected a week of Orderly Officer duties as punishment for my misdemeanour or, should I say, that of my fellows.

All of us living in the Mess were bachelors. On Saturday nights, a few of us regularly went to the Haunch of Venison in Salisbury for dinner. On one such occasion, we had a gunner officer, Graham Wallace, in our party and had to take him back to the Gunner Mess at Larkhill. On going down the hill to the Mess, he announced that there was a bit of a kink in the road where upon Dickie Bird, the driver, turned round to verify the message. The car left the road and ended upside down in an adjacent field. David Caton, Graham Wallace, and myself found ourselves sitting inside on the roof.

On emerging from the wreck David, with his cap pulled down over his eyes, exclaimed "Christ, I'm blind." We found Dickie Bird on the deck, spinning one of the wheels. A few minutes later, a white police jaguar rolled up. Out got a Sergeant asking "Everything alright gentlemen?" "Yes," we said, as Dickie continued to spin one of the wheels. Satisfied that no one had been injured, the police officers returned to their car and drove off disregarding the fact that we were all as pissed as newts!

For some, romance was in the air. Prior to this epidemic, none of us had the slightest interest in women except perhaps by way of finding a partner for the inevitable Mess dance. One by one, to a total of three, fell into the trap, and weddings with guards of honour, swords, etc., were all the rage. I caught the bug and became number four, which was the first major mistake I had ever made!

We were too young at twenty-five or so years of age, and I should have known better, bearing in mind my earlier time in the Indian Army, where one could positively not consider marriage before thirty – a most sensible rule! Looking back, mixing marriage with soldiering was a hopeless situation. Both lost out. Living remote from the Regiment in the village of Shrewton was disagreeable. To avoid the possibility of the Clyno breaking down during the morning run to Perham Down for first parade, I bought a Lambretta that fitted nicely in the back seat. There is a long hill on the A303 from Amesbury towards Tidworth, Beacon Hill. Provided I could get a good run at it, the Clyno managed the ascent. One morning, the police stopped me for no particular reason on the steepest section. Having satisfied the interest of the two officers, the Clyno kept stalling as I attempted to continue the trip. I had to turn round, go back to the bottom and start again.

A particular jolly I foolishly volunteered for involved taking part in a night exercise for RAF aircrew down behind enemy lines. We were taken to the south of Salisbury Plain in a covered truck, dumped out with a 1:250,000 map of the South of England (uselessly small scale) and a compass the size of a sixpenny piece, but with not the slightest idea where we were except south of the Plain. The aircrew among us were to make their way north to the Tilshead area, where they would be met by an agent. Another subaltern and I followed suit, as one of several pairs. The briefing advised that the 1st Battalion of the Lancashire Regiment, representing the enemy, was in bivouacs in the centre of the Plain and should be avoided at all costs.

We set forth in a northerly direction and in due course heard voices! We crawled around on the floor intending to conceal ourselves and somehow bypass the voices. No such luck – a burly Lancastrian Sergeant's boots appeared in my sight and that was that. We were escorted to a Company HQ under canvas, and once inside it we found ourselves in front of a table behind which was the Company Commander. Before he could utter a word I upturned his table and shouted "Go" to my mate standing beside me.

We ran into the darkness and came upon a row of Bren Gun carriers, found the key in an ignition, hopped in and drove off to a chorus of shouts and a lot of Anglo Saxon! For the most part, the Plain is motorable so, despite the darkness, we carried on without lights until at what seemed a safe distance. An hour or so later, we ran into another lot of voices but too many of them and were well and truly captured. We were taken to a POW cage, a wired place from which there was no way out.

Come the dawn, there was breakfast adjacent to a few large caravan type vehicles housing interrogators. While sitting on a jerrican, and just starting into a good English breakfast on an upturned oil barrel, one of them came down his steps, moved towards us, and kicked the plates out of our hands – my mate's first, mine second! We were then taken up the steps for the nasty bit. It was a night to be remembered – exhausting, intimidating, humiliating, cold, wet, and every other 'orrible thing. An experience but in hindsight great fun.

Each year, we endured the CID inspection of vehicles as well as the annual Administrative Inspection. The CID was conducted by a team of civilians in white coats whose job was to check the armoured vehicles for efficiency of maintenance. The vehicles had been painted and made spick and span in all respects. I recall one of the team tightening a loose track guard and noting on his mill board 326 track guard bolts loose. The bogies (wheels) had grease nipples on both sides so that grease could be applied from the outside of the bogies, whether fitted on the right or the left hand side. He discovered that we hadn't applied grease to both the outside and inside nipples, and that resulted in another negative report. The CID inspection was an exasperating experience.

After a year with No. 2 Troop, I was appointed Regimental Signals Officer, which involved managing the regiment's wireless communications. I was a bright choice for the job, bearing in mind that I was deaf in one ear! But that was known only to me!

Shortly after getting into the business of wires, fuses, and what not, the east coast suffered greatly, due to flooding from the sea to an extent previously unheard of. Off we went to a barren, foresaken place called Shoeburyness to set up communications for a Squadron employed to build walls of sandbags to stem the tide. Having established the wireless network it was a matter of all hands to the pumps. We all filled sandbags from near dawn to dusk. One day, with an alarmingly high tide, the water started to swill around our feet. A Royal Navy landing craft appeared, and we were taken off to a Minesweeper parked a mile off-shore. I have never before, nor since, been so cold. On reaching the vessel, we climbed up a net to get on board. Once inside we were stripped naked, given a change of clothes and a tot of rum – a great Naval tradition! Following a good night's sleep, a hearty breakfast, and our clothes returned neatly laundered, we were taken back to jolly sandbagging. We had been on a ship commanded by none other than Commander Kerrins of Yangtse River fame.

I recall being summoned to the Commanding Officer's office, where he offered me the opportunity of transferring to an Engineer Squadron engaged with the Mau-Mau operation in Kenya. The appointment was Motor Transport Officer (MTO). There was no compulsion about it, the decision to accept or decline was left to me. I had been married a matter of months and it didn't seem fair to desert the nest. But I was wrong – my second major mistake! That opportunity could have been a turning point in my career and for the best. Another big mistake made worse when George Palmer endorsed the error I had made.

Some while later, I was moved to the Regimental HQ as Assistant Adjutant. In that office, next door to the CO, one was privy to all sorts of goings on and quickly learned to keep ears open but mouth shut! The CO, Dick Barron, was a splendid chap. He had been a Squadron Commander with the Regiment for the D-Day landings and relished the policy of retaining armoured engineering in the Royal Engineers. In that endeavour, he fought tooth and nail with the top brass who, from time to time, sided with the Royal Armoured Corps. Everything he did promoted the Regiment's specialisation. He managed to move the venue of the annual RE Demonstration from Chatham to Sidbury Hill outside Tidworth, where representatives of all departments of the Army together with a colourful gathering of foreign military attaches would assemble to see what the Corps of Royal Engineers could do. It was exciting to be involved in all of that.

– 10 –
Fortress Engineer Regiment
Gibraltar, 1953-57

The prospect of my first posting abroad being in Gibraltar was quite exciting and the moreso on account of flying in an aeroplane recently 'retired' from the Queen's Flight. The interior was rather like a bus, two seats on one side and one on the other with limited head-room due to luggage racks, except when standing in the aisle.

We took off from Stanstead at an ungodly early hour and in the dark, calling at Bordeaux for a drop of fuel and at Seville because the airstrip at Gib was closed due to high winds. This was a fortunate stop-over causing us to be put up in the Reina Christina Hotel, one of the finest in the city. Sadly, there was no opportunity to see the sights and take-off was again at an early hour but with an unusual breakfast in the open at the airport consisting of ham, cheese, fresh fruit and, believe it or not, a carafe of red wine!

On boarding the aircraft and being technically minded, I was concerned on observing a pool of oil on the deck below one of the engines. It seemed indiscreet to draw attention to the oil. Besides my confidence had been fortified with quite a lot of red wine. Take-off procedure proceeded without interruption and a short time later we were very high over the unmistakable Rock of Gibraltar.

The hotel to which we were taken and in which we were to spend a few weeks was grim. It had all of the characteristics of a tired boarding house in Bognor; wallpaper falling from the ceiling, a loo (down the landing) the plumbing of which needed urgent attention, a bath badly stained with dripping taps, and so on. The atmosphere in the dining room gave pungent notice of the menu. Not an appropriate place for a 'gentleman officer' but that was his lot made worse by the Levanter, a cloud which frequently hangs over the Rock creating an unpleasant degree of humidity.

The appointment was Second-in-Command of the First Fortress Squadron Royal Engineers, one of three squadrons forming the Fortress Engineer Regiment, located in a fine Victorian barracks with a wonderful outlook to Spain and the sea. The job involved the management of four small power stations buried deep within the Rock and providing electricity for the Naval Dockyard twenty-four hours a day. A myriad of tunnels exists within the Rock, and to begin with it was necessary to be accompanied by an NCO familiar with the place to avoid getting lost! In due course, one learnt the geography and the thump-thump of the diesel engines could be heard and felt some distance away.

Each generator site had a rest room and kitchen, where the shift on duty could relax, while keeping an eye on the output indicators and listening to the sweet running of the engines. Each site had a large diesel fuel tank supplied by pipeline from a point on the surface. A regular weekly chore was the measuring of the quantity of fuel in the tanks. This was done with a most unusual dipstick, comprising a number of short sections bolted together which was tossed over and into the tank, there being little space above the tank to the roof of the tunnel. The 'opened' dipstick was then raised and lowered until it could be heard to 'bottom', then withdrawn and the level read off. This messy procedure was done several times because, not surprisingly, every reading was different! The results were then averaged and logged.

I recall an occasion when a Ministry auditor arrived on the Rock to check all fuel records and to ascertain the stock. We toured the sites together and dipped the tanks. Having completed the exercise, the funny little man asked, "What about the fuel in the pipes?" I dismissed the question, saying, "The pipes are always full and have been for years." But that wasn't good enough. Next day, the NCO in charge of each site had to measure the linear distance from delivery point to site and the bore of the pipe (which varied) before calculating the quantity of fuel therein. News of this little episode spread quickly through all departments of the Royal Engineers on the Rock, causing much amusement.

Some days later, the little man was faced with half a dozen huge pyramids of coal, which he decided to measure by pacing the base and estimating the height before calculating the quantity within the cone. Just as he finished what was considered a most inaccurate assessment compared with the exercise on the diesel oil, a D4 bulldozer started up and moved forward, pulling an enormous wooden crate from under one of the coal stacks, which promptly collapsed to about two-thirds of its previous height! When the embarrassed little man asked the reason for this arrangement the Warrant Officer in charge of the yard said, "Oh, they all have a hollow core, it assists drainage and reduces the possibility of combustion!" Little man went away not amused.

After a year I was appointed Adjutant of the Regiment and moved to a fine office next door to Dai David, the Commanding Officer and overlooking the docks. Dai David, a bachelor, had previously served in India. He was a stickler for detail. It was the custom every Saturday morning to inspect a quarter of the regimental area, the buildings, what went on in them, the sapper's barrack rooms, and so on.

This busy programme was undertaken by the CO, the Adjutant, and the Regimental Sergeant Major. Inevitably, there were things needing attention and it fell to me to make notes and subsequently draft a report for corrective action.

The CO would, for instance, enter the Ration Store, point to a commodity and ask the Rations NCO "What is that?" pointing to a portion of butter. The NCO confirmed that it was butter! The CO would then ask, "Why that quantity?" Reply – "Because that is the issue for the day." "How do you know?" "Because it is the amount required in accordance with the ration scale." "Where is the ration scale?" "In this book." This question and answer ritual was applied everywhere we went, and it certainly kept all concerned on their toes. As a result, everything about the regiment was checked each month. It was a good system and meant that come preparation for the annual Administrative Inspection, little needed to be done.

We had a troublesome NCO in the Headquarters. He would return from lunch, having had far too much to drink. It was reported that he had knocked up an unpaid bill in one of the bars in the town. Further investigation revealed that he had handed over his identity card by way of security for the debt. He was charged, and following arraignment before the CO, was arrested for court martial. It was my job to appoint a Defending Officer and to present the case for the prosecution.

Anxious to get rid of that NCO, I studied the Manual of Military Law, drafted my case in much detail, and called as a witness the Landlord of the bar in question. At the conclusion of the court martial, with a verdict "Reduction to the Ranks", the Presiding Officer congratulated me on my case for the prosecution, adding that I would have made a good solicitor!

The proceedings of court martials are always submitted to higher military legal authority for approval. Some weeks later, a letter arrived from the Adjutant General's Office, Ministry of Defence, in which it was stated that the Prosecuting Officer had been unnecessarily vindictive in dealing with the accused, and his attention should be drawn to that opinion by his CO.

The other two squadrons of the Regiment were Construction and Tunneling, and I have a tale to tell of both. The Construction Squadron was building the Princess Mary's Hospital, a fairly long-term project. In accordance with the drawings, it was necessary to excavate to 5 feet or thereabouts for the footings. This was taking some doing, bearing in mind that the sub-grade was rock! Well into the job involving much sweat, the supervising Ministry Engineer started to question the extraction of rock that was to be replaced with concrete. Signals passed to and fro before the necessity for this seemingly uneccessary work was resolved.

Meanwhile, a number of dump trucks were proceeding back and forth while disposing of the waste (rock!) over a one hundred foot high cliff into the sea below. The sapper drivers drove up to the edge and stopped against a baulk of timber before tipping the load. This was a boring routine, and one day, a sapper driver thinking of Christmas or something, went a bit too fast and jumped off his dumper as it mounted the timber and somersaulted down and down to the sea.

The Troop Commander decided to enlist the help of a naval acquaintance who agreed to dispatch a Boom Defence vessel from the dockyard in order to recover the dumper lying in about four fathoms of clear blue water. A diver went down, fixed a steel wire rope to the dumper, and signalled "Haul away".

A few minutes later, a main axle with two large wheels appeared on the surface while the greater part of the vehicle remained on the seabed. The recovery was eventually completed if only in a number of separate pieces.

The Troop Commander was grateful. He had a dumper needing major repair instead of the more serious matter of a dumper lost at sea. But that wasn't the end of it. The wheels of bureaucracy at the Dockyard turning however slowly eventually spewed out an invoice for some hundreds of pounds, addressed for the attention of the Commanding Officer, Fortress Engineer Regiment! The CO rang the bell for his Adjutant and said, "Sort this out"! It was duly sorted over a few lunch time drinks in the Naval Headquarters.

The men in the Tunnelling Squadron were all National Servicemen and Durham miners. They had huge hands and were incapable of standing to attention. Their hands faced forward instead of tight against the sides of their legs! They refused to refer to their Troop Sergeants as such, preferring the expression Shift Boss! For all that, they were a great asset and very proud of their specialised role.

By and by, the RSM was posted away and to my surprise was to be replaced by a Warrant Officer who had been my Troop Sergeant in 26 Assault Squadron at Perham Down. This was very good news, since I knew him well and knew also that he would be enormously helpful in the business of attending to soldierly aspects as well as those technical. We introduced a regimental parade routine on Saturday mornings, following the CO's inspection.

In due course, we raised the standard of drill on the barrack square to such an extent that the Regiment was fit enough to participate in the Ceremony of the Keys, a big historical occasion on the Rock. It dates back to the Great Siege of Gibraltar (1779-1783) and was inaugurated by Sir George Eliott, defender of the fortress, with a view to lessening the risk of the Fortress being captured. He ordered that the three main gates should be locked half an hour after the evening Time Gun fired at Retreat from the Signal Station. All aliens had to be out of the Fortress by then, and the gates remained locked until Morning Time Gun.

The infantry and gunner regiments on the Rock had long since provided the Escort to the Keys. I set about arranging for the Royal Engineers to fill the commitment. Following many rehearsals, the Fortress Engineer Regiment undertook the ceremony and it was am impressive performance in front of His Excellency, The Governor, and the public, who considered it an important social occasion. I was very proud of all ranks who

> By Command of Her Majesty Queen Victoria her Royal Engineers, who since 1716 had comprised a Corps of Officers only, and her Royal Sappers and Miners, who since their formation as Soldier Artificers at Gibraltar in 1772 had been Other Ranks only, were constituted into one Corps, the present Royal Engineers, on the 17th October, 1856.

Origin of the Corps of Royal Engineers.

> To celebrate the Centenary
> of that Occasion
> Colonel D. M. Eley
> and the Officers, Royal Engineers
> request the Honour of the Company of
>
> at a Sherry Party
> in the Peterborough Chambers
> on Friday the 19th October, 1956
> from 6.30 o'clock to 8.30 o'clock.
>
> R.S.V.P.
> Mess Secretary,
> R.E. Officers' Mess.

Celebrating the formation of the Corps of Royal Engineers.

rose to the occasion in a superb fashion.

At the time of the Suez crisis, a number of ships carrying the troops, their vehicles, and equipment arrived in the docks en route to the Suez Canal. Amongst the naval officers was a Lieutenant Commander hell bent on playing polo. Dai David, having played polo in India, got to meet him, and together they decided to organize a polo match on the Campamento just inside the Spanish border. Yours truly was enlisted to find the necessary number of horses.

The only horses on the Rock were those harnessed to the carriages used to ferry tourists off the cruise liners around the places of interest. I negotiated with a dozen or so of the drivers that we might borrow their steeds for the game. In due course, the horses were moved to the polo ground in Spain on the arranged date and time.

I had never played polo, but never mind, I could ride and joined the Fortress Team as Number 4. We had a great game against the Navy. One thing led to another when it was discovered that a pre-war polo fund had been frozen ever since. The Governor arranged for the fund to be reopened so that the sport could be introduced once again.

Dai David and I bought a proper polo pony in Spain named Coco-Cola and formed a team that subsequently took on the experts from Jerez. By the time I left Gibraltar, polo had been firmly established and is, no doubt, played there today. I don't think I ever hit a ball, but it was fun trying to do so! Instead, I became most useful by riding down on an opponent so that he was denied the opportunity of scoring a goal.

During my time in Gibraltar, no Royal Navy ship passed without calling for fuel, a run ashore for the crew, and so on. Ships were adopted by the regiments when in port, and this led to many opportunities to exchange entertainment and enjoy a spell at sea. The Regiment had three such associations, one with the cruiser HMS *Ceylon*, another with the destroyer HMS *Barossa*, and another with the submarine HMS *Surprise*.

I took a few sappers on board HMS *Ceylon* for a memorable one-week experience at sea, during which the ship participated in an exercise. There were three ships representing a battle formation, the cruiser, the destroyer HMS *Apollo*, and an oiler named MV *Tide Reach*. Away out in the Atlantic, we were engaged by a submerged submarine that fired green flares indicating a torpedo fix. Bearings on the flare were recorded and a subsequent investigation revealed whether or not one of the ships had been hit.

I did a watch in the night with one of the officers and envied the responsibility as we sailed on with no navigation lights. When a change of heading was required, the order was given to the other two ships by the illumination of lights. At one stage, a merchantman appeared on the horizon ablaze with lights. As our courses converged, it was necessary to show conventional lights. The merchant ship quickly responded and disappeared.

On one of the mornings, the Padre was transferred to *Apollo* in the Bosun's Chair, i.e. along a steel wire rope connecting the two ships, the tension being applied by sailors as in a tug-of-war. Standing on the bridge, I found the routine rather amusing as the Padre made his way across a quite turbulent sea. The Captain, noticing my amusement said, "Right, you're next!" On arriving on *Apollo* I was greeted by a Mess Steward holding a silver salver with glass and a bottle of brandy.

In the case of *Barossa*, I joined the ship's company for amateur dramatics and took part in a play. We got to know the Ward Room officers very well on several return visits. On a particular visit, we arranged games ashore and dinners at soldier/seaman, NCO/Petty Officer, and officer level. The association with the Royal Navy was strong. It was said on the Rock that the RAF did the typing, the army did the work, and the Navy set the tone!

The morning following one of those dinners I was making my way to the office and noticed that the regimental flag was absent from the flag pole. On enquiring of the Commander of the Guard why it was not in its proper place, he didn't know. When I arrived in my office, the CO rang the bell, "Why is the flag not flying?" I didn't know, but said steps were being taken to find it. He then took me by the arm to the window from which we watched HMS *Barossa* proceeding out to sea with the RE flag fluttering from the mast.

My two days on board the submarine *Surprise* was a rare opportunity. I joined the boat at 6 a.m. and was met by the Captain in blue pants and a white Arran pullover. He was two years younger than myself. He asked if I had had breakfast? I had not, so he said, "Follow me". We climbed the conning tower and descended to the Ward Room that was a very small space indeed. He then said "Scotch, Brandy, or Gin!" The boat submerged at 0900, and I spent the rest of the two days being introduced to what goes on in a submarine, submerged and on the surface – a fascinating experience.

Having left the wretched hotel we moved to rented accommodation in the town named '49 Steps' because access was just that! After six months of climbing 49 steps, a family with a Quarter high on the Rock offered us their basement accommodation that was surplus to their requirements. It was just three, small empty rooms with independent access, affording us free accommodation while waiting for a Quarter.

During this time Ma and Pa paid us a visit traveling to Gibraltar in the P&O Cruise ship *Oriana*. It was exciting for me watching for the arrival with my binoculars. When the ship appeared, I rushed off to the docks, having arranged with the Agents to go out to meet them in the Tender. We had great fun touring the Rock, meeting the famous apes that run wild all over the place and slipping into Spain for enjoyable suppers in the various bars at La Linea. On one evening, we went to a Club to watch flamenco dancing. Pa thought it was hilarious. At the conclusion of their visit, we drove home to the UK in our recently acquired Ford Prefect, enjoying night stops in Spain and in France.

With few military Quarters on the Rock, one accumulated points while waiting for a vacant Quarter. We waited eighteen months before being allocated a fine house in Roger's Road, a few minutes walk from South Barracks. The back of the house overlooked the dockyard and the Moles, where visiting ships were berthed. When HRH Duke of Edinburgh visited the rock, the Royal Yacht was in dry dock below the bathroom window from which I observed the Duke having his constitutional morning walk while shaving. The rooms were spacious with a vast kitchen 'below stairs' that conjured up days of servants. Bringing cooked meals up to the dining room was a pain. So much so that I arranged for a lift, a large box with shelves that was operated with a rope.

Our servant, Anna Garcia Fernandez, lived in Spain and walked 3 miles to the Quarter each morning and 3 miles back at the end of the day. Anna, just twenty-six years of age, had five children looked after by her mother while she was at work. We visited her and her family at their home at Christmas each year. They had a tiny house built by her husband mostly of corrugated iron! It was bereft of water supply, sanitation, electricity, and everything she was accustomed to seeing and using in the Quarter. We were very fond of Anna, who not speaking English, taught us all the Spanish we needed!

When the time came to say good bye, she brought a pencil drawing of a house with a long drive and a gate house. It transpired with the help of an English speaking Spanish Clerk in the Headquarters that Anna assumed we lived in a large house in England with a long drive. She and her family wanted to come home with us and live in the gate house! She was quite serious about this proposal and was deeply disappointed when we explained that it could not be. On her last day, she left the Quarter waving and in floods of tears before trudging off home. It was a sad moment.

In our last year, I was studying for the Staff College entrance examination. The Governor, Sir Harold Redman, assembled the dozen or so officers similarly engaged and suggested that we accompany him on a battlefield tour during which we would study the Penninsular War as had been set for the exam. During a two-week romp, we visited La Caruna, Salamanca, and Badajoz, the sites of three battles during the campaign. Each officer was required to research an aspect of one of the battles beforehand and be prepared to direct the party on the battle site. The history of the War was well chronicled in the Library in Gibraltar and that facilitated the research. Having seen the situations encountered by the English Army under the command of Sir John Moore (who was killed at La Caruna) and the allied Spanish troops, and noting that in many instances things had not changed much, we felt exceptionally well-prepared for the exam! In the case of Badajoz, for instance, the breach in the city wall remained unchanged as a large heap of stones and masonry.

The social life on the Rock was the more enjoyable on account of being on familiar terms with senior officers as well as our contemporaries, e.g. The Fortress Commander, the Admiral C-in-C Mediterranean and the Air Officer commanding at the North Front airfield. Each of these officers had a beach hut on the shore at Catalan Bay, all three in a row with their appointments displayed on each hut! No one was permitted to walk the beach in front of these huts. Instead, one had to climb a great many steps in order to pass behind the huts and get down to the other end of the beach.

Mess parties took place all through the year, and the Rock being only 5 miles long and ¾ of a mile wide, everybody got to know each other very well indeed. I recall a party with a difference at the Admiral's residence on the occasion of a visit by a Portuguese warship. There was a speed restriction of 5 knots within the Moles beyond the docks. On arriving, the Captain of the Portuguese ship, ignoring the restriction and moving far too fast, ploughed into the stern of HMS *Eagle*, an aircraft carrier preparing to return to the UK for Christmas. The hole in the back of *Eagle* would have allowed access by a London bus. It was rumoured that the Admiral on board *Eagle* was at the 'heads' (the loo) at the time of the impact and narrowly escaped injury during the incident. On arriving at the party, it became known that the Captain of the Portuguese ship had been relieved of his command and had been returned to Lisbon by air! Next morning, while shaving, I watch a huge piece of steel plate being welded over the hole in the stern of HMS *Eagle* which set sail for the UK later same day.

Incidentally, the C-in-C Med at the time was Admiral Foster-Brown, who on his retirement joined Eamon Andrews' TV programme "What's My Line?" We invited him to dinner in the Mess at South Barracks, together with his Flag Officer.

After dinner, one of the games we played involved turning a sofa onto its back. The contestants then ran forward placing their bums on the seat of the sofa thus righting it. However, some didn't make it and arrived on the floor with a bump! One such person was the Chief Engineer David Elly who having failed to right the sofa was flat on his back gasping for air and very red in the face. Someone rushed forward, undid his tie, and raised him into a sitting position. At that moment the CO asked me where the Admiral and Flag were? I searched the Mess but could not find them: they must have left.

Next day at coffee break, we played the tape recorder traditionally used on Guest nights to record the proceedings during and after dinner. When we got to the bit about the sofa game and David Elly's bump, a voice was heard to say, "Christ, he's dead, I'm off"! That was Admiral Foster-Brown.

Another senior naval officer I knew was Captain Myers (known as Crap Myers), then Captain of HMS *Bulwark*, who as a submariner had won a Victoria Cross during the Second World War, having taken his boat through a minefield and boom defences into the harbour at Taranto in Italy, torpedoed a number of Italian warships. I met Captain Myers having arranged a Dinner Night with the Number 2 on board *Bulwark*, the ship then being fostered by the Regiment during its stay.

After dinner, Dai David and Crap Myers ordered pints of beer. Emptying their pint beakers was the signal for two teams, one naval, the other sapper, to dismantle iron frame bedsteads assembled either side of a narrow companionway between two Ward Rooms. The object of this exercise was to move the dismantled bedsteads through the companionway, from one room to the other, the winning team being the first to present a reassembled bedstead! Well, imagine the situation in that companionway as six sappers, myself included, and six naval officers strove to move their dismantled bedsteads through the companionway. It was bloody mayhem! I emerged from the fracas less shirt and somewhat bruised, as were all those involved, but the Sappers won the day much to Dai David's satisfaction! Captain Myers was subsequently appointed Admiral C-in-C Med. My tour in Gibraltar was one of the most enjoyable of my entire career. At the end of it, I was posted to the Officer Cadet Squadron RE, a return to the School of Military Engineering at Gordon Barracks, Chatham.

– 11 –
Office Cadet Squadron RE
Chatham, 1956

The role of the Cadet Squadron was one of training intakes of National Service officers for a period of sixteen weeks after which they would be posted to units at home and abroad. We had all sorts to deal with, and a few of them in each intake were half way through engineering degree courses at university. Our job was to cram as much information about field engineering into them as possible in the short time available. Additionally, the syllabus included the rudiments of administration, a good deal of square bashing, and an introduction to Mess routine in their own Mess.

Instruction on dry and wet bridging was my lot. This was achieved in the class room and during practical exercises. Initially, I enjoyed instructing but the repetitive nature of it, intake after intake, soon palled. It was obviously important to maintain the momentum and this was done by revising the lecture notes and the exercise situations. Doing so involved a great deal of work at home, since most of the day time was occupied instructing.

One of my wet bridging exercises ran continuously over two days, including the night, involved building a Bailey bridge across the River Medway. The Medway is a tidal part of the Thames estuary. The bridge building was assisted by a Coles crane, a fairly large crane mounted on an equally large vehicle. While the crane was being operated below the high water mark, it broke down. All efforts to repair the fault failed, and a few hours later the vehicle was in deep water with its electric mechanisms ruined. Thankfully, the incident was attributed to the exigencies of the exercise. Someone somewhere must have had a problem but I never got to hear about it.

The highlight of the course for the cadets was, of course, their Passing Out parade, which was attended by mums, dads, girlfriends, and sometimes wives. The parade was accompanied by the Corps Band, with an inspection and address by a senior officer. There followed a church service, after which relatives were entertained in the HQ Mess. The entire programme followed a standard procedure, relieved only by our being allocated different responsibilities on successive occasions. Chatting to the relatives about their 'ewe lambs' and how well they had done, whether or not they had done well, required a bit of imagination!

During the previous week, each intake put on a show at which incidents during the course were remembered, the idiosyncrasies of the instructors and staff included. Some of the shows were exceptionally good when, for instance, the intake happened to include a few natural comedians.

The Malayan campaign (terrorists) was on-going at this time, and a few cadets from each intake were posted to that operation. On returning home, they would often pay us a visit. It never ceased to amaze me how they had developed. Young inexperienced chaps for the most part had, in such a short time, become mature men. For them, National Service had indeed done them a service. In that respect it was rewarding to have been involved in the process.

I can't say that I enjoyed my time in the Cadet Squadron. The repetitive nature of the routine got me down. I missed the regimental life terribly, the association with soldiers applying their expertise to the various jobs in hand. I longed to be back with the armoured regiment and the routine in Gibraltar where every day presented new challenges of one kind or another. That depressed state of mind led me to consider an alternative occupation in the Army. There were two options – A Long Transportation Course (Railways) or a Long Survey Course (Land Survey). I chose the latter.

My decision was strongly opposed by the CO of the Regiment of which the Cadet Squadron was a part. Field engineering was all he knew and he could not understand why I should wish to depart from it. However, I made my decision, and following a few telephone calls, got a place on the next Long Survey Course. I was warned that promotion above the rank of Major was unlikely but, at the time, I didn't much care about that. I just wanted a change and training for a particular technical type of work leading to a job which I would enjoy. It was a correct decision for me, as was to be confirmed during the rest of my career.

Before being accepted for the course, I was summoned to the HQ of the Military Survey Department in London. I remember fitting myself out for the occasion with bowler hat, umbrella and brief case! Not the custom seen nowadays in the city but very much the norm in my day.

– 12 –
School of Military Survey
Newbury, 1958

There were nine on the course at Newbury in Berkshire, four British officers, two Canadian officers, two Nigerian civilians, and one British civilian. On account of my rank, I was appointed Class Senior (Dog's body!). During a period of eighteen months, we were expertly trained in all aspects of land survey including the application of photogrammetry (aerial photography), geodesy (the nature of the planet and the control of land surveys), astronomy (positioning on the earth's surface), cartography (the presentation of surveyed information), and printing (the production of maps and aeronautical charts).

It was a fascinating programme heaped with interest and in all ways exactly my cup of tea. We had tremendous fun on the course – lots of practical work as well as the theory and the satisfaction of achieving positive results from trigonometrical and mathematical solutions. The great thing about the solutions was that they were either right or wrong – there is no grey area, nothing in between.

We were a course of quite different characters and persuasions. The Canadians were naturally very pro-Canada. They compared just about everything in the UK with Canada, the latter being better, of course! The British civilian spent much of his time thinking how he would crack the last few clues in the morning's newspaper crossword. He always had a mini-chess set at hand. The Nigerians were a bit aloof. When there were stores and equipment to be carried to waiting vehicles, they always disappeared to the loo! We presumed that they felt it undignified to be seen carrying things! But we eventually changed that attitude. During an exercise involving a long hike across Dartmoor with aerial photographs for navigation, one of the Nigerians (for whom I was responsible) lay down in the lee of a huge boulder and announced "Hari, I can go no further."

It was getting dark and Dartmoor can be an angry intimidating place. I hoisted him to his feet and propelled him along, ignoring his acclamations. On another occasion, I was measuring a line on the ground with a steel tape with the same chap assisting. I was on my knees while he stood watching. It was raining. I said "Get down here and help hold this tape" to which he replied

"Hari, I am not military and when I go home I will supervise, others will hold tapes and carry things."

The course led up to an Estate Survey, which each of us undertook independently on farms in Devon. The work took about three weeks, making observations by day and doing endless calculations by night. This final work entailed everything we had learned and was presented as a hand drawn map, supported by all of the observations and calculations. A successful job earned us exemption from the final written paper of The Royal Institution of Chartered Surveyors (RICS), the Institution recognising the quality of the training. To actually obtain the qualification, it was necessary to undertake a practical task at some later date.

I made many friends at the School and have remained in touch with most of them. At the end of the course, we were posted all over the place. For me, the appointment was Officer Commanding No: 22 Map Production Squadron in Cyprus, the squadron being one of three in 42 Engineer Survey Regiment.

There was no rush to meet the joining date, so instead of travelling by air I took four weeks leave and we drove there instead. Caroline, being just eighteen months, the family thought we were mad! Much time was spent planning the route and the list of essentials. One of those was a case of Heinz Tomato Sauce, since Caroline would eat nothing unless splattered with the sauce. The car was a Morris Oxford station wagon, which I converted into sleeping accommodation with curtains on the windows. A few nights were spent in B&Bs in order to have baths and deal with laundry.

The route, prepared by the AA in the form of a set of flip-over sheets, took us through France, Italy, the length of Yugoslavia, into Greece and hence to Turkey on the south coast of which we took a ferry from Mersin to Larnaca, Cyprus. I can't remember how many miles but it was a long haul with little time for sight-seeing. Nevertheless, we became aware of the various cultures and the varied environment along the way. It became progressively warmer and was extremely hot at the end.

The miles through France and Italy were uneventful. In Yugoslavia, we had to be careful as the country was controlled by the military. The consequences of straying off the main highway could have serious implications. Camping out in the sticks was not recommended. We were encouraged to park overnight in what they called International Camp Sites, mainly for long distance haulage. On a few occasions, we didn't reach our planned destination and took the risk, me on the floor outside, mum and daughter locked inside!

It so happened that the north-south 'Autoput' (motorway) was being constructed beyond Zagreb and not before time with the state of the roads as they were. I suppose for reasons of economy, the new road was being built on top of the old. This meant travelling short distances on a finished macadam surface but, for the greater time on very rough surfaces, sometimes exceptionally so. It was necessary to look out for the changes – there being no ramps one risked a resounding bump and the possibility of damage. Where minor roads would eventually cross the new highway the bridges had been built in advance. They stood like pagodas and looked very strange.

At one point high in the hills, the road simply disappeared. There was evidence of road construction plant having been at work but not a soul in sight. It did not seem possible to drive over the terrain such was the size of the stones lying everywhere and the depth of the ruts. We stopped. I got out and walked ahead for half a mile or so to the crest. Before me lay a hutted camp with all manner of road building materials, plant and vehicles and, I was glad to see, people! I walked on.

By and by, I reached the camp and got talking to a chap who did not, of course, understand a word of what I was saying! I dug out a piece of paper and by means of illustrating my predicament caused a broad smile of comprehension to break across his face. He hollered at other chaps who, gabbling away, joined the conference. Next, one of them jumped onto an enormous bull-dozer which fired into life and moved off in the direction of whence I had come. After an hour or so, a reasonably flat surface was created making it possible to rejoin the road. His reward was a generous tumbler of scotch. We were in the middle of nowhere and well north of Belgrade.

On reaching Belgrade, we found the official camp site a few miles outside the city and set up shop. Mum and daughter went off to the shop in search of a coke. Shortly afterwards, a blue-suited gentleman arrived, accompanied by a grey suited colleague. We shook hands and exchanged greetings – the one in the blue suit spoke English perfectly. The grey-suited figure said nowt. The ensuing conversation ran along lines of "Very much hope you are enjoying yourselves in our country" – "Where are you bound?" – "What a fine motor car you have", etc.

Having mentioned the car, the guy in blue opened the driver's door and sat in the seat. "Very smart," he said, before running his hands under the seat, opening the glove box and generally having a thoroughly good look over everything. "It really is a splendid car." He then got out, shook me by the hand, wished me well and went off with his colleague, who had not uttered a word.

It seemed strange to me that a couple of intelligent-looking professionals should be visiting a camp site? Mum and daughter returned with the question "Who were your visitors?" "Haven't a clue," said I. "Well, they have just driven off in a large black chauffeur driven limousine." So that was it, I thought. We had been checked.

On reflection, this was not surprising as tourism in Yugoslavia at that time was a non-event and my passport, examined on entry, showed 'Government official' instead of 'Army Major', for obvious reasons. The Intelligence people in Cyprus subsequently concluded that our vehicle registration number would have been checked and reported from every camp site, and that the two visitors had almost certainly popped out from the Ministry in Belgrade to have a look at who was driving a smart British car and camping in Yugoslavia, e.g. a senior military person and his aide.

A few days later, and north of Skopji the road, though dusty, was in fair shape. I had become accustomed to driving miles without sight of man nor beast and unexpectedly going through a small community – a few dwellings, a shop and a tree in the shade of which there was usually a policeman with a motor cycle. In one such instance, I was going a bit fast and spied in the mirror a policeman on motorcycle following equally fast. I pulled over and stopped as he came alongside. There was a bit of "Parlez vous anglais?", "No", "Sprecken ze deutch", "No", followed by exasperated silence. He then took out his notebook and drew a circle, adding within it 30 MPH! "Ah," said I, "Ah," said he, before waving me on with a flourish of his notebook.

On attempting to cross the frontier into Greece I was denied departure from Yugoslavia, as I hadn't spent enough money. Visitors were required to spend a specified amount per day while in Yugoslavia and be prepared to prove it with receipts. I had some receipts, but not enough of them. There was no way out, so I turned back about 20 miles to the last village and bought a quantity of food and a few useless things to make up the outstanding balance.

The journey through north-eastern Greece was uneventful until reaching the frontier with Turkey. We crossed the border without difficulty, but beyond it the road ceased to exist. Instead, I followed a track with woodland either side and in the middle – a farm track. After a short distance, I came upon a barrier across the track, which I assumed indicated the Turkish frontier, and beside it a sentry box, but no sentry or anybody else in sight. Blowing the horn failed to attract attention. With some apprehension, I raised the pole that was the barrier and drove on cautiously, imagining that at any moment we would be apprehended.

Once clear of the woodland, I saw a Turkish flag flying from a pole adjacent to a modern building about a quarter of a mile ahead. On reaching the building, outside of which then stood a couple of uniformed officials, I got out and offered my hand of friendship which was grasped and well shaken. This was a relief.

One of the officials then got excited over Caroline. We didn't understand what he was saying but he clearly meant her well as he picked her up and made a tremendous fuss of her, while the other official checked passports and the car's Carnet de Passage. It was a most friendly interlude. I subsequently learned that the absence of a decent road between the two frontier posts reflected longstanding disagreements between Greece and Turkey and infrequency of border crossing at that particular place. With regard to the unmanned barrier, the new frontier post had replaced it but removal of the old must not have seemed necessary.

We drove on for a few days to Istanbul where, finding no camp site, I decided to seek advice at the British Embassy. The Embassy was in a busy street behind tall and firmly locked gates. In the wall at the side, I found a window which I tapped a few times. It was opened by a man who had all of the appearances of a Sergeant Major though in plain clothes. He looked me up and down before inquiring the nature of my business. I asked my question about camp sites to which his response was "Are you British?" I thought I looked fairly British and to prove the point handed him my passport. We then had a useful conversation, during which he recommended 'no camping' and a hotel instead. I could park the car in the Embassy compound! Having collected overnight essentials, we walked to the hotel and enjoyed a refreshing meal and a good night's sleep. Regrettably, time was marching on and there was no time for sight-seeing in that vast and interesting city. We went on our way the following morning.

Nothing much happened during the trip down the length of Turkey. We camped at each stage of the journey and, in due course, reached the port of Mersin on the south coast from which a ferry would take us overnight to Larnaca in Cyprus. According to our paperwork, there was a sailing on that particular day, but the harbour was empty – not a ship in sight. It was unbearably hot, which affected Caroline in so far as she lay on the back seat, a limp perspiring mite!

While considering our next move, a very large bald-headed man came walking towards the car. "Are you expecting the ferry?" he inquired in perfect English. "Well, it won't arrive in the port until around eight o'clock. That being the case, you might care to relax in my garden in the shade and with some refreshment." It was 2 p.m. and the thought of hanging around for the next six hours was unpleasant, to say the least. The offer was accepted and off we went, following his car.

A substantial residence stood in a spacious garden of shrubs and trees. Once seated around a table, a maid appeared in black dress, white apron, and hat! Tea was ordered, and while waiting for it, we chatted about our journey and destination. He asked whether or not our papers had been processed. They hadn't. It was then suggested that much time could be saved later if we took our papers (passports and carnet) to the appropriate office in the town.

I went off with him on foot along several streets. The office appeared to be closed but he knew better, and on banging the door with his great fist a sleepy young clerk opened it and we went in. Another clerk who had been enjoying the siesta moved himself, and following a brief conversation with my host, produced a tray of rubber stamps which were duly applied to the papers. We returned to the house by another route, calling at another office, where I was able to purchase tickets for the ferry. During the walk, I learned much about Mersin, its history, and its architecture. I discovered that my host was of Yugoslav origin and a grain merchant. He had left Yugoslavia at the end of the war, having got on the wrong side of the authorities there.

On returning to the garden, we had more tea after which it was suggested that we make the acquaintance of the crane driver at the port. The ferry, not being of the roll-on roll-off type, the car would be raised and lowered onto the deck. A word with the crane driver would ensure that he was ready for the job and would place the car on the foredeck. He was a pleasant enough chap and responded enthusiastically to my host's instructions. I gave him some lira, which was welcome! We returned once more to the garden.

At 6.30 p.m. or thereabouts, a siren sounded – the ferry had arrived. We collected our things and drove off, following our host back to the port, where the crane driver was ready and waiting. As we were going to sleep in the car, there was no need to carry anything on board.

Our host beckoned us to the gangway, saying he would introduce us to the Captain. There didn't seem to be anybody of importance whom he didn't know. We parted with our tickets and climbed a staircase to the bridge of the ship, where we were introduced to the Captain, who ushered us into his cabin. Glasses and brandy were produced. The Captain had little English, so the conversation was relayed back and forth by our host, who obviously was well acquainted with the Captain! The welcome completed, our host shook hands warmly and after profuse thanks on my part, escorted us to the car, then on the deck, and left with a cheery wave.

A short time later, the ferry slipped its moorings for the final stage of the journey. A pleasantly cool breeze was a welcome change, compared with the stifling heat endured during the day. The car was made ready for the night, much to the amusement of some passengers! On entering the ship's dining room, the head waiter approached. "Do you have a tie, Sir?" I found a tie with some difficulty, not having worn one for the past few weeks.

We arrived off Larnaca about 8 a.m. It's not a deep water port, so passengers and all else had to be transferred ashore in a succession of large boats. I was intrigued about the method to be used for the car until one of the boats appeared with stout timbers straddling its gunwales, specially for me! All passengers were assembled in the lounge for immigration formalities. One of the ship's officers asked me if I had locked the car, which would be taken ashore shortly. I had. Watching through the windows I saw the car hoisted high over the side, twisting one way and then the other. Quite suddenly at the appropriate stage of the twisting, it disappeared! A few minutes later I saw it safely on the planks and on its way.

In due course, we boarded one of the boats and were taken ashore. It was not a very large harbour at Larnaca, and looking in all directions I couldn't see the car. I walked towards the entrance to the port, found an office, and asked where the car might be.

It was round the corner some distance from the harbour wall. I was puzzled as to how it had got there since it was locked. It was attracting a good deal of attention from a number of officials, including Cypriot police. The rear nearside window had been smashed. I was ushered into the office and asked to produce identification. Having explained why I had come to Larnaca and where I was going in Cyprus, the tone of the questions changed from one of extreme suspicion to a degree of understanding. A statement of what I had said was presented for my signature after which I was able to proceed out of the gates and on to Zyygi Camp, the location of 42 Survey Engineer Regiment.

It had been a most unpleasant couple of hours since disembarking from the ferry. While driving towards Zyygi, I considered how the car had become such a focus of attention. A few days later, I was summoned to an office at the HQ Middle East Land Forces, where I met up with one of the policemen from Larnaca in the presence of a couple of the HQ staff. During a comprehensive discussion, it transpired that some illegality had occurred, probably that something planted on the car in Mersin had been removed during the transfer from ship to shore, or immediately on being placed ashore. The car, then unlocked, had been moved to where I had found it.

Piecing everything together, there had been ample opportunity for the planting while I was walking the streets of Mersin. The precise circumstances of the incident were never discovered, not to my knowledge anyhow, but they seemed to explain why we had been made so exceptionally welcome on arriving in Mersin the previous afternoon by a total stranger.

– 13 –
42 Survey Engineer Regiment
Cyprus, 1960

Zyygi Camp was located in the middle of nowhere, equidistant from Nicosia and Limmasol. The soldiery and unmarried officers lived at the camp, the married officers, Warrant Officers, NCOs and some soldiers, were in quarters in Limmasol. A couple of ancient buses collected us in the morning and returned us to our quarters in the evening. It was a most unusual situation and not very satisfactory, as it generated a 'we' and 'them' attitude which, as I was to discover, was a recipe for trouble.

Having met the CO, Adjutant, my officers, Squadron Sergeant Major, and senior NCOs, my immediate requirement was khaki drill uniform. An Indian gentleman was summoned to measure me up for shorts, shirts and KD service dress. I must tell you a bit about him.

He was clothed in white with turban, and as far as I could see, had just one tooth in his head. He and a couple of colleagues, plus their wives, had served the Regiment while in Palestine. They not only provided a tailoring service but had a shop, under canvas, where they all lived and where one could purchase just about anything given a day's notice! When the Regiment was moved to Cyprus, the CO sent for these people to thank them for their sterling service and to bid them farewell.

On arriving at Zyygi Camp, the Regiment's vanguard was amazed to find the camp followers at the gates! How they had got out of Palestine, never mind crossed the sea to Cyprus, was a complete mystery! However, there they were and there they quickly re-established themselves in the service of the Regiment.

My uniforms must have been made up during the night because the first fitting took place on the day following the measuring process. And the alterations were minimal.

The resources of the Regiment were such that land could be surveyed from aerial photography, computations completed, and a map produced. That was, of course, why the unit was there, i.e. in support of Middle East Land Forces (MELF). Once settled into the routine of the Regiment, I felt comfortable in my new role.

My squadron comprised a Headquarters and two Troops – A Cartographic Troop (Drawing) and a Print Troop, both commanded by officers with appropriate experience in cartography and printing. The NCOs and sappers were similarly skilled. The Squadron Sergeant Major (SSM) was a splendid chap. Although a skilled cartographer, his role was 'regimental', with responsibility for discipline and the management of the men in the squadron. In those respects, we enjoyed identical aspirations, e.g. soldiers first, technicians second! With his support, I quite quickly introduced morning parades, weapon training, map reading, and other activities that had not been uppermost in the mind of my predecessor.

That change of emphasis revealed an element of resistance in the ranks. One morning, while taking the parade, I noticed a small stone a few feet from where I was standing on which was painted an eye with eyebrows! On consulting the SSM after the parade, he explained that there was a disgruntled group of National Servicemen in the ranks and that from time to time there had been incidents causing disquiet.

In one such incident, a CND Ban the Bomb motif had appeared in large black paint on the gable end of one of the barrack blocks. The stone, I had observed, was a minor expression of the disquiet, the first since my arrival and best ignored. A short time later, when the Regiment was assembled in the gymnasium for an entertainment, the CO arrived to an audible 'hissing'! Next morning, I called together my officers, the SSM, and all senior NCOs, to consider what seemed to me outrageous and totally unacceptable behaviour that should not be condoned. It was not known who precisely was leading this culture but a few within the ranks were suspects. I was advised that one reason was almost certainly the fact that come 4.30 p.m. daily, Monday to Friday, a majority of officers, warrant officers, and NCOs boarded the buses for Limassol and the comforts and facilities of their homes, leaving a minority of junior officers and junior NCOs in the Camp, remote from the pleasures enjoyed by those quartered elsewhere. This was perpetuated throughout weekends. It was a difficult situation but that reason was understandable.

Why this situation had been allowed to continue, I could not understand. I decided the best thing to do was to address the squadron on a special informal get-together, draw attention to the incidents that had occurred prior to and since my arrival, explain my reasons for finding the situation unacceptable, and offer an opportunity for those responsible to seek redress of their grievances free from threat.

As anticipated, there was no response. However, I had made my position clear and had left all concerned in no doubt that any further incident would be thoroughly investigated with a view to revealing the identity of those responsible. I suspected that the junior NCOs billeted at the Camp knew very well who was at fault but felt unable to blow the whistle for fear of the consequences.

Fortuitously, one of the National Servicemen thought to be involved came before me on a charge of insubordination, involving one of the NCOs. It was beyond my powers to deal with the circumstances of such a charge, so I referred him to CO's orders, where he was sentenced to 28 days detention. In the normal course of events, he would have been detained at Zyygi Camp. Instead, I arranged for him to serve his punishment with an Infantry Regiment at Nicosia, where the facilities for detained soldiers were more satisfactory. On returning to the squadron the sapper before me was a changed person! The action taken had been a salutary warning to all ranks.

Sometime later, a Regimental Cadre of sappers was formed for the purpose of training selected men considered potential junior NCOs. I put the offending sapper forward. He won selection and was promoted Lance Corporal.

In a further attempt to rid the squadron of the unacceptable behaviour and consolidate the situation, the SSM organised regular recreational activities. These had been overlooked in the interests of technical work. We involved all ranks in that development, with the object of fostering better relations. I believe this altered attitudes significantly especially since activities were arranged over weekends.

I have recorded this saga as something of importance. Never before had I experienced a situation verging on mutiny. The actions taken from the onset of the problem undoubtedly raised morale and reduced the unavoidable and adverse effects of personnel being separated during off duty hours. Moreover, attitudes amongst the NCOs seemed changed. Discipline all round was sharper. Priorities afforded to technical work had in some ways poisoned the routine. The result was a great improvement overall.

– 14 –
Headquarters Middle East Land Forces
Cyprus, 1961

After a year with the Regiment, I was transferred to HQ MELF at Episkopi to work as a Staff officer with responsibility for on-going mapping, as required for the Middle East area of operations. I had moved from the production of maps to the management of map requirements, employing the resources of the Regiment. The office had a small staff – Deputy Director Survey (Colonel Brian Irwin), Staff Officer Survey 1 Captain Doug Arnott (Administration), Staff Officer Survey 2, myself, and Map Research Officer (Civilian). I was assisted by a Staff-Sergeant and a Corporal.

The daily routine started with 'Morning Prayers' in the Colonel's office at which time incoming mail, signals, among other matters of business were considered and responses agreed. Any on-going priorities for mapping were also considered. This was an excellent arrangement as all of us became aware of the matters at hand.

One morning, we considered a signal from MOD advising us that the Director of Military Survey, no less, would visit us on such and such a date. We wondered why and sent a signal requesting clarification, reason for visit, and what he might wish to see and do. The reply from one of his Staff Officers was to the effect "D Mil Svy wants a rest – so do we"!

British Embassies worldwide have map libraries. In the case of the Embassy in Tehran (Iran), we were asked to visit and review the map holding that was thought to be a bit superfluous to requirements, e.g. obsolete maps. I flew to Tehran, where I spent a thoroughly enjoyable ten days staying at the residence of the Military Attache, a sapper Colonel, and working at the Embassy by day. At the end of the job, I had consigned a large quantity of obsolete maps to a bonfire and had listed up-to-date replacements that would be sent in due course. I attended a number of social occasions and was privileged to meet several senior Iranian officers. At the same time, I was well briefed on the political situation in Iran, which was immensely interesting.

Supreme Headquarters Allied Forces Europe (SHAPE), based outside Paris at the time, had subordinate commands covering the whole of Europe, e.g. AFNORTH (Norway), AFSOUTH (France), AFCENT (Naples), AFMED

(Malta) and a few others. The Deputy Director was responsible to AFMED as a technical adviser for mapping and aeronautical charting. It fell to me to visit Malta fairly regularly and that too was enjoyable. I flew from Nicosia to Benghazi (Libya), to Tripoli (Libya), and hence to Malta using a regular European Airways flight. Not surprisingly, AFMED was staffed by Royal Navy officers, and we had a few enjoyable 'runs ashore' in Valetta and elsewhere on the island. The work involved the discussion of policy documents drafted for ratification at subsequent conferences at SHAPE.

During my tour of duty, there was another organisation (subsequently disbanded), namely Central Treaty Organisation (CENTO) based at Ankara, Turkey. I accompanied the Deputy Director to Ankara on several occasions and got to know him very well. We stayed in the same hotel and enjoyed dinner together at the end of the day. As was the case in Tehran, there were receptions and the opportunity to meet Turkish officers and their wives.

On one such visit shortly before Christmas, our Turkish hosts suggested that on concluding business we might like to do a bit of Christmas shopping. An English speaking Captain in the Turkish Army was assigned to give us a guided tour. Off we went and having visited a few large stores, which offered nothing of particular interest, we were taken through a small door in a very large factory type of door and into Ankara's Red Light District! Initial reaction was one of embarrassment as two British Army officers were taken on a tour of a great many brothels – near naked and voluptuous women, none of whom were in the least way attractive – waved at us with fruitless encouragement. We were glad to get back through the little door but thanked the Captain all the same.

I took a fancy to sailing. The Nuffield Trust provided the Joint Services Yacht Club with Albacore and Firefly dinghies. Although I had sailed on the RE yacht *Overlord*, it was a 30-square-metre vessel, and my experience as crew was no match for single-handed sailing in a Firefly. A member of the Club taught me the ropes, and before long I was taking part in Point Series racing.

In gorgeous warm weather it was such a pleasure to race or just potter about in shorts, nothing else, so much so that I would be found at the Yacht Club most afternoons until 4 p.m., when we all repaired to the bar until about 6 p.m. During the summer months, work started at 6 a.m. with a break for breakfast at 9 a.m. Work stopped at 1 p.m.

During another of Ma and Pa's visits, Pa reckoned Cyprus was the Army's playground! At that time there was no emergency situation, that came later. Ma and Pa, who had traveled to Limassol on a cargo boat, the *Egyptian*, stayed in a house we rented for them, but for most of the time stayed in our quarter.

By and by, the Deputy Director (Brian Irwin) was appointed Commodore, and a vacancy arose for the Secretary's post, which I was more than happy to fill. From that point on, we more or less ran the Club. His wife, Audrey, managed the bar. By the end of my first sailing season, I was very dark brown in appearance, the result of sunshine and salt water.

Tom Labey, based in Aden, was not very well. The Deputy Director thought it would be a good idea if I paid him a visit, which I did, flying with the RAF in a Hercules from Nicosia. Unfortunately, two of the passengers were Alsation dogs, and during a long direct flight, they dropped their guts from time to time on the floor of the aircraft. The odour was appalling and did little to encourage me to open my ration box provided courtesy of the RAF. That and the fact that Hercules are extremely noisy, made for a pretty unpleasant trip.

Tom's map library was in the hell of a mess and that worried him. It was another example of hoards of obsolete maps stored in a damp and dusty shed. Putting it right was to be a big job far exceeding the resources available in Aden. All I could do was appreciate his situation and report back on my return to Cyprus.

During my visit, we sailed on his yacht in the Gulf of Aden. That was very enjoyable in warm sunshine, but the threat of falling overboard into shark-infested waters occupied my mind more than a little, as I lay at leisure on the deck and far beyond the nets that protected swimmers.

The return journey to Cyprus was far from straightforward. The only RAF flight available was destined for Lyneham (UK). The Captain of the aircraft thought it would be possible for me to take a flight from Lyneham to Nicosia without much delay but I didn't think it would go down very well in the office were I to find myself stuck at Lyneham en route from Aden to Nicosia!

The flight was scheduled to stop over at an airfield in Libya to collect personnel for UK. I decided it would be best to disembark there and hope for a flight to Nicosia before too long. That was a big mistake! I was marooned in the Libyan desert day after day, watching and waiting for one of the many arrivals that would take me to Cyprus. It was a very boring interlude, and I regretted not having taken the opportunity via Lyneham.

Successful completion of the Long Survey course in 1960 was recognised by the Royal Institution of Chartered Surveyors (RICS) and allowed me exemption from the written examination. There was time at this stage to turn my attention to the outstanding practical survey task that would qualify me as an associate member of the RICS. I decided to undertake a plane table survey at a scale of 1:25,000 of an area north of Limassol. I spent many enjoyable hours humping my plane table and tripod legs over the area that was fairly remote and rugged.

On one occasion, it was necessary to extend my work beyond an escarpment. I needed to walk to the top and did so following a goat track at a gradual angle of ascent. The steep ground over which I was walking was loose crumbly shale and rather unstable. A short distance from the top I slipped, losing my footing, and tumbled down and down. My descent was very fortunately interrupted by a small tree preventing me from continuing a considerable distance to the bottom. I had already suffered a few scratches and bruises and had it not been for the tree, my situation a long way from help might have been a lot more serious.

In 1962, an Assistant Director Survey (AD Survey) post replaced that of Deputy Director. Colonel Brian Irwin went home to take up an appointment in the Ordnance Survey Headquarters, at Southampton, and I was appointed AD Survey in his place. Doug Arnott and I continued to run the office at HQMELF in much the same way as had been done previously.

However, the political situation in Cyprus took a turn for the worse, with a resumption of trouble between the Turkish and Greek Cypriot inhabitants. A nasty situation developed, so much so that the United Nations intervened. This was unpopular as the General Officer Commanding the military in the Sovereign Base areas and his staff felt perfectly capable of managing the situation. As the situation deteriorated with a number of terrorist type incidents, the Ministry of Defence decided to withdraw all families from the island.

A United Nations force arrived (UNFICYP) in a succession of aircraft. The families were returned to the UK in the same aircraft. The UN force, mostly British, wore blue berets and most unfortunately the British Major General in Command and the Major General in command of the military within the Sovereign Base areas didn't get on. They had been at the same school and their distaste for each other had become common knowledge.

In order to deal with the insurgency, in so far as it affected the Sovereign Base areas, the GOC set up an Operations Room that was manned twenty-four hours a day. During daylight hours, it was managed by the GOC's staff, but in the dark hours, it fell to me to take charge. There were three desks, my own in the middle with an RAF officer on one side and a military officer on the other. There was an elaborate communications set up – telephones, radio and fax machines operated by a few NCOs through which information was received fairly continuously from MOD UK, from UNFICYP, and from the various units dealing with situations as they arose. The three of us considered incoming signals and information and responded appropriately. Everything was logged and the wall map displays were maintained up to date. On a few occasions the GOC would appear for a briefing on the current situation, sometimes accompanied by the Air Marshall in command of MELF. Those visits were always intensely interesting, providing an opportunity to listen to senior officers discussing necessary actions, issuing instructions and responding in the case of MOD UK.

On several occasions, a signal received from MOD UK made it necessary to set up a conference, using the communications set up. MOD would ask a question. A response was considered. A draft response having been agreed it was transmitted. We then waited while the response was considered in UK, and a short time later, a further communication would be received and the process continued. Those conferences could last nearly an hour.

During this period of unrest, I had occasion to fly out to Ankara on a mapping matter. It was a standard Middle East Airlines flight (MEA) as had been used previously when I accompanied Brian Irwin. On returning to

Nicosia late at night, I found the staff car waiting to take me back to Episkopi had a Turkish driver. During the ninety minute journey, we came upon a number of check points usually manned by Greek Cypriots. These people had no authority and they were armed.

Initially, we just stopped and passed the time of day, but at one such check point both the driver and myself were invited to get out of the car! Standing by the car in the dark and more or less surrounded by a gang of armed ruffians was one thing, but their reaction on opening the boot and observing my suitcase with an airline tag marked ANK on the handle was quite another. I was more concerned about the well-being of the Turkish driver than myself as he gabbled away in argumentative discussion with one of the Greek Cypriots, since I had no idea what they were talking about. I said little beyond explaining that I was on my way home to Episkopi, but conscious of the fact that I was in plain clothes and unprepared to discuss the reason why I had been in Ankara.

Moving very cautiously, I got back into the car and instructed the driver to do likewise. I then, through the open window, shook the hand of the chap seemingly in charge of the check point and told the driver to start the car and move off slowly. For the next few seconds and minutes my imagination as to what might then happen was a bit worrying. We drove on in silence, preoccupied by a somewhat shaking experience.

Having moved out of the Quarter and sent the family home, I was accommodated in the Mess of the Scottish Infantry Regiment at Episkopi. I can't remember the name of the regiment but I think it was the Cameronians.

The HQ MELF Mess was next door and on the occasion of formal dinner night the absence of an invitation from the Air Marshall and his lady wife to the CO of the regiment displeased the CO's officers. Their discontent caused them to assemble outside their Mess and proceed round and round the MELF Mess loudly singing 'Colonel Bogey'! We learnt next day from one of the guests that the rendering competed effectively over the music being played during dinner.

In spite of the emergency, social life continued unabated within the Sovereign Base areas compared with the war footing adopted by UNFICYP. During this time, I busied myself converting an obsolete ¼ ton army trailer into a camping facility. During the evenings four of us played a lot of bridge to pass the time when not on duty.

One of the four was the Staff Officer at HQ MELF, a Lt Col previously Indian Army. One day, on returning from work on my practical task, I found him at the door to the Mess. Observing my plane table, tripod and my dishevelled state he enquired "And where have you been?" In the course of explaining what I had been doing I revealed that I had been beyond the boundary of the Sovereign Base area. Bearing in mind that a couple of officers travelling between the Base areas at Nicosia and Episkopi had met up with undesirable people and had been killed, he forbid me to continue my work beyond the Base boundary. My practical task was thus brought to an abrupt and unfinished conclusion.

At the conclusion of my tour of duty, I gave a farewell party in the Mess for my friends and contacts. The invitation sent to all and sundry from the Air Marshall, the GOC, their staff officers and wives requested dress in 'Bad Taste'. A good number of guests turned up wearing Blue berets! The party ended on a beach where we all swam and revelled into the night under a full moon.

Instead of flying home to the UK, I took a ferry from Limassol to Trieste with car and camping trailer on board. It so happened that the CO of the infantry regiment was also returning to the UK. We had a most relaxing and enjoyable four-day trip. On arrival in Trieste I proceeded to Innsbruck in Austria in time to meet the family arriving by air. We drove back to the UK, camping along the way.

– 15 –
Ordnance Survey Scottish Region
Edinburgh, 1964

My next appointment was Regional Officer Scottish Region OS. Prior to the war, the OS was a military organisation reflecting its defence connotations. Few people bothered with maps compared with the post war period when travel, leisure and holiday pursuits, turned national small scale mapping into a multi-million-pound business.

On the conclusion of hostilities, a great number of surveyors were demobilised and returned to the OS to continue their pre-war work as civilians. On the other hand, however, the directing staff were military officers, Royal Engineers. The Director General, for instance, was a regular serving Major-General. The assistant directing staff in charge of the various departments were Lieutenant Colonels and some subordinate staff were Majors. Relationships within the organisation were excellent reflecting a continuation of military traditions and procedures.

The Headquarters at this time was in a hutted camp near Feltham, rather like one of those hastily constructed military hospitals. It was some years before the HQ moved to its splendid purpose-built building on the outskirts of Southampton.

The Scottish Region office was in Rose Street, Edinburgh, above Paddy's Bar. The staff comprised of an Assistant Regional Officer (Captain RE), a Superintendent (formerly a Warrant Officer RE), two experienced surveyors, an Executive Officer (Civil Service) and a small civilian clerical staff. The Region was divided into 6 sub-divisions; at Melrose in the Borders, at Perth, at Inverness, at Aberdeen, at Glasgow, and at Edinburgh. Each of the divisions was in the charge of a Chief Surveyor who controlled the activities of the surveyors engaged on survey tasks throughout Scotland.

The job in hand was the revision of the pre-war 1:2500 scale mapping. This was being conducted throughout the UK, including Northern Ireland, with a deadline for completion by 1980, i.e. 'The 1980 Plan'. At the same time the 1:1250 large scale mapping of urban conurbations was being updated.

The surveyors were provided with images of the original maps contained in a map case. By observing new detail on the ground, in relation to previously surveyed detail shown on the original image, it was possible to add the new detail by 'running' lines and measuring angles and distances from the old to the new. The result was a revised manuscript image that was passed to HQ, where the revised map was produced.

The revision entailed transferring the new detail to a thick glass plate carrying the old image and coated with a substance that could be scribed. The scribed information with name plates and conventional signs was then photographed. The original and revised information could then be combined photographically and converted to a printing plate for the production of the revised map. A proof copy of the revised map was then passed to the Region office for proof-reading and the registration of any further changes, after which the map went to bulk production.

Apart from managing the activities of a large number of surveyors through the Chief Surveyors, my job was to co-ordinate those activities with a view to the completion of the revision throughout Scotland by 1980. My first interest every morning was to note progress on a small scale map of the whole region displayed from floor to ceiling in my office. This was updated daily.

I visited the various Chief Surveyors regularly and thus became very familiar with Scotland, notably remote areas in the west, the north-west, and the north. During each visit I had the opportunity of meeting the surveyors at work, appreciating what they were doing, responding to queries, and dealing with personnel matters. High morale was of crucial importance, especially in remote areas where they were working in difficult terrain and in adverse weather conditions.

During the revision of the more remote areas to the west, I found that the time taken by the surveyors in getting to their work was disproportionate when compared with the time actually on the job. Access over moorland and mountainous areas was difficult. During the annual conference of Regional Officers, I suggested that a great deal of time could be saved had we the use of a helicopter. This was agreed in principle subject to costs, etc.

On my return to Edinburgh, I sent an exploratory letter to a number of firms operating helicopters, including British Airways. The response was almost immediate with offers to meet me for discussion of the employment I had in mind. In each case, it was suggested that meetings take place over lunch. During the next few weeks, I accepted invitations to meet representatives on different dates at the Café Royal in Edinburgh. Once I explained the need for helicopter assistance, the duration of the work, and the areas to be visited daily, the representatives went off to prepare contracts. The proposals when received were sent to HQ with my recommendations, taking account of the service offered in detail. In due course, one of the proposals was considered acceptable, and I was authorised to proceed with the arrangements.

The firm concerned sent one of their pilots to a rendezvous in the highlands. We flew over the terrain and worked out a plan for the most economical use of the helicopter on a daily basis. The pilot was a splendid chap on leave from

Nigeria, where his normal role was ferrying the President and other senior administrators from place to place. We established a base for the pilot and his machine at an hotel to which the surveyors would travel daily by car. Having supervised the employment for a few days, during which a regular procedure was adopted, I handed the task over to the Chief Surveyor.

On a subsequent visit to the hotel, one of the surveyors, claiming to represent them all, explored with me the hazard factor while being flown over the highlands and the possibility of some remuneration. This was a tricky situation and one which if not resolved could jeopardise the whole arrangement. We agreed to kick the matter into touch but to review it through the Union representative at HQ. As I expected, the matter was raised at HQ but the negotiations were not finalised until the work involving helicopter transport had been completed.

Inevitably, the helicopter was on the ground between morning and evening trips. Aware of this, it was suggested that tide lines along the western coast might be photographed, using infra-red film that would show water in black and the adjacent terrain as a normal image.

The survey of tide lines was a most labour intensive operation, due to the fact that the line of the high and low tide could be observed during a very short period of time. The work had been done previously by locating poles along the edge of the water and fixing their positions at leisure from known positions along the coast.

The possibility of photographing the tide lines from the air had obvious advantages. A special camera and film arrived from HQ. We removed the door on the co-pilot's side of the helicopter, and with the camera mounted on a short length of timber, I was able to view the terrain and the sea as near vertical as possible through the view finder. We practised this on the ground before strapping me into my seat and taking off to reach approximately 1000 feet above mean sea level.

While observing the ground through the viewfinder, I was able to advise the pilot to go left or right until the tide line was more or less vertically below. By making over-lapping exposures, we were fairly confident that the images could be assembled to present the line of the tide over a considerable distance. There were two problems – noise making communication between myself and the pilot difficult and the cold with me exposed to the elements.

Having spent two trial sessions at appropriate times I sent the films to HQ for processing. The images showing the boundary between water and dry land were acceptable, but it was not possible to recognise detail on the ground from which to fix the tide line with the necessary accuracy. The flying of tide lines was aborted, but it had been good fun doing it!

John Bartholomew, son of the well known Scottish map publisher, always welcomed me for discussion about OS policy for Scotland. He had continued to publish maps at various scales based on original pre-war OS plates given to his business by Sir Winston Churchill in return for the use of their printing facilities during the war, when defence and other wartime needs exceeded the resources of the OS.

As the firm did not employ surveyors it was assumed that their maps were updated using copies of revised OS maps. There was obviously some commercial competition in this respect but since the content and presentation of Bartholomew maps was different compared with the OS equivalents their practice that might otherwise have offended copyright was discreetly ignored.

John, Chairman of the Scottish Geographical Society, frequently invited me to meetings of the Society, when OS policy was often debated, indeed criticised, by members who considered the OS Scottish Region as their own Ordnance Survey! I was often invited to explain why the OS did this and didn't do that. As a result, I passed Scottish preferences for the depiction of detail to HQ OS for consideration.

The local authorities and public utilities relied extensively on 1:1250 large scale maps for planning and other purposes. When on tour in the Region, I always made a point of calling on local Planning officers in the vicinity of my itinerary.

For a visit to Kirkwall in the Orkney islands, I flew from Edinburgh on a flight bound for Lerwick in the Shetland islands. Having got into conversation with a fellow passenger, I was unaware of having landed on Orkney. The Stewardess interrupted our conversation to verify that I was travelling to Orkney and having done so advised that we had been there for the past ten minutes!

I found a stack of One-Inch to One-Mile photocopies on a table in the Planning Officer's office. On enquiring what the copies were used for, he said they were sold to tourists and visitors at one shilling a time. This was a gross infringement of copyright that had to be discreetly put right.

I was frequently invited by various societies to lecture on the work of the OS in Scotland. Those occasions were always enjoyable and usually involved a meal in a local restaurant. At the end, I was always presented with a cheque payable to myself! However, on returning to the office in Edinburgh, the Executive Officer lost no time in collecting the remuneration – fees received were the property of the OS!

During the map revision process, the surveyors were required to record the gaelic names of all places visited. Any error in spelling on a published map could cause complaint. In order to verify the names collected by the surveyors I enlisted the assistance of the School of Scottish Studies in Edinburgh.

On my initial visit, I was surprised to find that the Director was a German! Sometime later, we had lunch together and that afforded an opportunity to discover how a German had been appointed Director of an important Scottish establishment. It transpired that he had been a prisoner of war on Shetland for several years and put his mind to learning the celtic language from the locals. After the war, he had decided to remain in Scotland, applied for the job and was duly appointed.

A most useful feature on any OS map is the alignment of the high voltage electricity network. Although depicted using a conventional sign changes in direction are surveyed providing a reliable reference point for navigation in remote areas.

Another contact was the Manager of the Scottish Electricity Board, whom I met from time to time to discuss developments. On the first occasion I observed that he worked in a comfortable office with a small round coffee table and a telephone – no In and Out trays, no files or other paperwork in sight! During a lunch, I remarked on the apparent simplicity of his managerial procedure only to discover that he verbally delegated all actions to his staff, knew little or nothing about electricity, and was an economist!

An annual event was the visit of the Director-General, usually accompanied by his wife. A most detailed programme was arranged in consultation with the Chief Surveyors. Dates and times were set for visits to surveyors at work, accommodation in hotels, opportunities to visit places of interest, etc. It was extremely difficult to stick to the programme, due to the amount of discussion that took place wherever we went. This resulted in surveyors hanging about in the middle of nowhere waiting somewhat disagreeably for the Chief. For the D-G and his wife it was a bit of a holiday with morale boosting and much technical discussion. All concerned breathed a sigh of relief when it was over!

– 16 –
42 Survey Engineer Regiment
Barton Stacey, 1966

Managing Scottish Region was a most interesting and enjoyable job away from things military for three years. After a spot of leave, I found mself appointed Second-in-Command of the Regiment that had returned from Cyprus and was based at Barton Stacey near Andover. Nearing the end of the tour of duty, I received notice of my next appointment in support of the US Department of Defense and promotion to Lieutenant Colonel to go with it.

I attended a senior officer's course during which the routine of command was studied. One such routine was the completion of confidential reports for the officers under command. The form provided space for a pen-picture of the individual concerned. The space occupied about ten inches. I remember a Brigadier advising us that it was quite unnecesary to fill the space when a few carefully chosen phrases would suffice. For example, he said, "I wouldn't breed from this officer!" and "He's good, you ask him!"

– 17 –
US Department of Defense
Washington DC, 1969

The posting to the USA was to present the most interesting and demanding job done during my service so far. I found myself wearing two hats, so to speak, because the job entailed two distinctly separate roles. On the one hand, I was the personal representative of the UK Director of Military Survey in the USA. On the other hand, I was in command of a UK unit named 512 Specialist Team RE, known in US Army circles as 512 SPECTRE.

Commander US Topocom inspects 512 SPECTRE on the Queen's Birthday.

512 SPECTRE was based at "TOPOCOM", the American name for United States Topographic Command. The role was to assist the Americans with the tracking of satellites, the results being used to improve the accuracy of mapping and aeronautical charting worldwide. For this purpose, the unit comprised Army surveyors and radar/electronic specialists drawn from the

512 Specialist Team, Royal Engineers.

Royal Navy and the Royal Air Force. As the United Kingdom did not at that time have the resources for the launching of satellites, but needed access to the observed data for its own mapping and aeronautical charting, the data was provided in return for the assistance given by 512 SPECTRE.

It was a small unit of 25 people, who with the exception of myself and my Second in Command, did a tour of duty of 6 to 9 months. Their tours were short on account of the nature of their work, which took them to some very remote places and involved working at all hours of the day and night.

We flew to New York, courtesy of the RAF and on to Washington next day. Shortly before we arrived, there had been riots in Washington. Anxious about our security, the chap from whom I was taking over the job, decided to find us an apartment some distance from the city instead of in the suburbs where he and his wife were living. It was a ghastly place, a recently built modern apartment block in a heavily built up area and totally unsuitable for all sorts of reasons not least of them most unsatisfactory for entertaining. Desmond O'Connor, who lived in Alexandria, Virginia, found us a residence in a leafy suburb called Tauxmont, with a spacious garden and a swimming pool. We moved in without delay!

Desmond became a particularly good friend. He was Australian and had come to the USA to take up a basic research appointment in everything to do with surveying and aeronautical charting. He was a very clever fellow and completed his career as Professor Emeritus of Perth University, Western Australia, having become a national authority on matters environmental. He found it frustrating to be hanging about at airports so he learnt to fly and leased an aeroplane for convenience! We sailed a lot in his yacht on the Potomac River, which flowed past the end of his garden.

There was an occasion when I accompanied him to New York on a business trip. He knew New York quite well and introduced me to an Irish Pub where we drank a good deal of Guinness and worked our way through a typical Irish menu. After that we visited Times Square at around two o'clock in the morning. Later the same morning, it was Sunday, being a good Catholic, he took me to the magnificent St Patrick's Cathedral. I followed him round kneeling when he was kneeling, lighting a candle when he lit one, and generally complying with his routine. On emerging from the cathedral he announced: "All clear for another week!"

It has been said, I think by Philip Duke of Edinburgh, that our two countries are divided by a common language. Common it may be, but I discovered a few embarrassing differences shortly after taking up my appointment. While drafting a letter in pencil, I made a mistake and asked Sheila Gore, my twenty-two-year-old secretary from Oklahoma, if she had a rubber. She replied "No, Colonel, but I can bring one tomorrow!"

As was customary, I was invited to a luncheon at the HQ of US Army Topographic Command where I worked. A US Colonel came to my office to collect me and escort me to the venue. Along the way on spying a Men's Room I asked my escort if I might spend a penny. He replied "No, Sir, you're a guest. You can't spend a dime!"

During that meal I sat next to my host General Podufaly, the General Officer commanding US Army TOPOCOM. By way of conversation, I mentioned that I had taken my family to see the National Archives, which I thought was a fitting thing for new arrivals to do, the archives comprising the originals of the Declaration of Independence, the Bill of Rights, and other documents relating to the early history of the USA. The General remarked that he had never seen the archives, which surprised me. A few minutes later he said "Harry, have you seen the Crown jewels?" "No Sir," says I, to which he responded "I've seen them five times!"

Attending receptions was a fairly common occurrence for the Brit at TOPOCOM. On one lunch-time occasion to be followed by a reception later the same evening, the lady to whom I had been speaking felt she needed to rest during the afternoon and hoped she would waken in good time. I suggested I might knock her up about five o'clock to which she replied with enthusiasm, "That that would be just marvellous!"

I gave an after work drinks party for the chaps in all three US services with whom I was working and meeting regularly. A Lieutenant Commander US Navy approached me during the party and asked had I got a dime. I didn't but queried why on earth he needed a dime. He said to call a cab. I said, "Leaving so soon?" "No, he said, "I need to get a drink!"

Prior to the successful Sputkik mission by the Russians, it was impossible to carry out survey operations across the oceans, i.e. employing triangulation on the surface of the earth, because one could not make theodolite observations across the oceans beyond the horizon. The internal surveys of the continents and sub-continents had, of course, long since been completed to varying degrees of accuracy using astronomy, but the position of one continent in relation to the position of another, e.g. Europe and North America, had not been fixed to an accuracy consistent with the requirements of aircraft and ships.

An example of these discrepancies was contained in a report from a civil airline pilot flying over the pacific. According to his heading and his chart, some small islands should have been seen on the starboard side of the aircraft in flight. However, they were seen on the port side! This is an extreme example. The islands concerned were uninhabited and insignificant and the linear discrepancy from 30,000 feet above sea level was equally insignificant. More importantly, the possibility of a missile arriving in the wrong place could not be tolerated. Consequently, there was international interest in producing a thoroughly accurate presentation of each and every place on earth. That was the mission and 512 SPECTRE was privileged to take part.

Surface triangulation for the purpose of controlling the detail depicted on maps is simply the solving of triangles using trigonometry. For instance, with a measured base and the observed angles from its extremities to a third point, it is possible to establish the location of the third point. Having solved that triangle one has two new base lines from which two more triangles can be solved, and so on, across the terrain being surveyed but not across the oceans since direct lines of sight cannot be observed beyond the horizon.

The launching of the Russian's Sputnik provided a fundamental change of procedure and solved the difficulty of making observations across the oceans. Instead of triangulating in the horizontal plane, it was possible to solve triangles in the vertical plane using a programme of observations to the satellite. In this way, the positions of stations many miles apart and separated by the oceans could be determined with great accuracy. This was a significant development in the business of terrestrial mapping and aeronautical charting.

During my tour of duty, 512 SPECTRE undertook satellite observations from stations on the island of Maui (Hawaii), Thursday Island (Queensland, Australia), Bermuda, Tierra del Fuego (Chile), Arica (Chile), the island of Shemya (The Aleutian chain west of Anchorage, Alaska), Thule (Greenland) and at Brownsville (Texas). It was my good fortune to visit my people in each of these places. There is a story to tell about each trip but I must be brief! These journeys are written up in chronicle order but they took place at different times over three years.

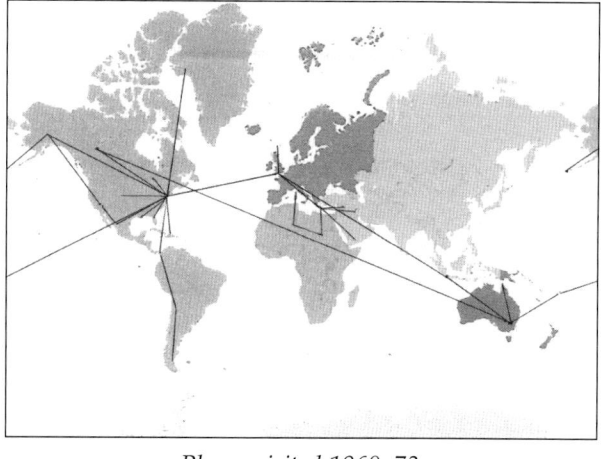

Places visited 1960–73.

By way of keeping the Next Of Kin of the officers informed about their sons' whereabouts and activities, we published a newsletter from time to time entitled SPECTRE (Specialist Team RE).

A copy was sent also to the Director of Military Survey in the UK and to my parents for their interest. It was an interesting newsletter complete with photographs. I much regret not keeping a set for myself.

Maui, Hawaii

The flight to Hawaii took off from Washington's National Airport, as did most flights to destinations within the USA. The posh Dulles Airport received and dispatched international carriers. National Airport had two runways in the shape of a X. While waiting for my flight, I noticed that aircraft were taking off along both runways on a sort of 'I'll go after you' basis. It looked alarming, and on taking off I found it positively scary, observing through my window seat an aircraft hurtling towards me and presumably missing my own by a not great distance.

I recall arriving in Honolulu with a few hours to lose before the short hop to the island of Maui. On checking into a hotel adjacent the airport, I felt sleepy, following a long flight, and concerned lest I would miss my flight to Maui. Anyway, I tipped the concierge who promised to wake me up in good time, which he did thank goodness! The trip to Maui was in a tiny aeroplane, so much so that I found myself seated next to the flight deck, if you could call it that, with half a dozen other passengers behind me. In a matter of minutes, we on the ground on Maui.

Maui, Hawaii, is a beautiful island, and anyone arriving there enjoys having a garland of flowers placed around one's neck as a welcome. In my case, the presentation certainly looked unusual over Service Dress uniform!

The hotel where I stayed had a gorgeous view over sand to the sea, with palm trees right and left bending in the breeze. The greeting from one to another on the Hawaiian islands is 'Aloa' and with it an extraordinarily warm welcome. Such a happy lot of people everywhere. During dinner, a quartet of steel drums entertained us. The chaps doing the job laid on a delightful beach party, which went on into the warmth of the night and a bit of the next morning! Maui was a lovely place in every way and I was quite sorry to leave.

Thursday Island

Thursday Island lies at the top of Queensland, Australia. I had attended a conference in London and took off from Heathrow for Sydney, via Singapore overnight. I found myself sitting next to a New Zealand businessman, who turned out to be great company. We enjoyed an excellent dinner after which lights were dimmed, and we were encouraged to sleep. My friend interrupted the process of being tucked up in a blanket, asking the hostess if there was any

Remy left in the bottle we had enjoyed after dinner. 'Oh yes', she said, whereupon my friend said, "why don't you bring it back and then tuck yourself up for the night!" We didn't sleep a wink, enjoyed the brandy and chatted about everything under the sun, hour after hour. On arrival in Sydney, we had breakfast together, shook hands and went our separate ways, sadly never to meet again.

Having collected my bag, I approached the exit where a dozen or more chaps held notices on card with the names of those they were expecting. To my surprise one such card was marked 'CRAWFORD'! Thinking there can only have been one Crawford on the flight, I went up to the Crawford card and found the chap holding it dressed in a smart chauffeur outfit. We confirmed that it was me he wanted to meet. He explained that the High Commission in Sydney had put his limousine at my disposal for the day until my evening flight north to Cairns.

Well, well, I thought, what a nice gesture. I spent the rest of the day touring Sydney and its environs, with everything of significance and importance pointed out to me. I gave my driver lunch mid-day.

The flight to Cairns took off in the early evening. I was met by John Underwood, the officer in charge of the party on Christmas Island. Before moving by road and ferry to the island, we spent a night in a local hotel. Having travelled from a chilly London, I was most unsatisfactorily dressed for the heat and humidity. I was glad for a swim in the hotel pool, followed by a late dinner and a comfortable catch-up sleep. Next morning, I completed my journey and spent the next few days watching the team at work tracking a satellite.

A while later, I arrived in Bermuda during a torrential rainstorm, never having seen anything like it before. Apparently, it broke all known records. The main form of transport seemed to be the bicycle, and there were very few cars. I stayed overnight in Hamilton and slept to the accompaniment of revelling on two cruise liners tied up to the jetty adjacent my hotel.

Chile

I had two teams operating in Chile: one at Tierra del Fuego, the southernmost island, which includes Cape Horn, across the Magellan Strait, and the other at Arica, in the north next to the boundary with Peru. The first leg of my journey took me to Miami, from which I took an overnight flight to Panama, arriving around 4 a.m. I had arranged to spend a couple of days with my friend, Colonel Gunter Ruthe, the American representing US Army Topographic Command in Panama.

On clearing the departure procedure, I was surprised and glad to see him there to welcome me. I remarked that I didn't expect to see him at such an ungodly hour! In reply he said "You would have done the same for me." True. He escorted me to a bachelor officer's quarter in the base where I had a good sleep.

Presenting a plaque to Colonel Gunter Ruthe, US Army.

The next day, he introduced me to the Chief of the Panama Canal, with whom he had arranged a VIP tour. It went on most of the day, starting with a briefing about the history and management of the waterway, followed by a chance to watch a couple of large vessels making their way from the Atlantic to the Pacific. It was a fascinating experience and all the more enjoyable on account of a long and splendid lunch. I felt very privileged.

Later that same day, I joined a flight for Santiago in Chile. Having booked into a hotel in the center of that bustling city, I had a rest from the long journey. The next morning, I was met by a Captain, Chilean Army, who took me to the Military Headquarters, where I was due to meet officers of the Geographical Department. That meeting was something of a reception. There were two general officers and a number of colonels present. None spoke much English, but my escort was fluent. During a couple of hours, seated around a large table laden with delicious food and wine, I explained what I needed to do and how I wished to do it.

Although the sites for observations had been approved through diplomatic channels, relations between Chile and the United States were not good, due to the President currently in office (Allende) having confiscated the Annacondi Mines from American ownership. Although that was a political upset of little concern to my hosts, it was nevertheless necessary to play down the fact that I was undertaking a US mission. This ruse was exemplified by the arrangements for the importing of the equipment from Washington. It was packed in wooden

With the Manager, the Panama Canal.

The Varicella *navigates the canal.*

crates, prominently marked as if of UK origin with stencilled images of the Union Jack and shipped to Santiago via Argentina!

Having established very good relations with all present I sat down with my escort, the Captain, to plan the programme of activity that would take place on arriving at Punta Arenas. I was to fly from Santiago, while he for some strange reason travelled half the length of Chile overland.

HQ Chilean Geographic Ministry, my escort on the right.

The next day, my escort collected me from the hotel to go walkabout in the city centre and enjoy lunch together. This was an opportunity to get to know each other, and for me, to learn a few things about Chile, its military influence, the political situation, etc. My escort was in uniform – grey in colour and reminiscent of German uniform. On crossing a busy street with traffic moving in both directions, I noticed that he stepped off the pavement regardless of the traffic which slowed to allow us safe passage! We parted, having fixed our date and time for the rendezvous at Punta Arenas.

Later that same day, I took a taxi to the residence of the Naval Attache, who had left a message at the hotel, inviting me to dinner. I had never met him – another example of the hospitality afforded to visitors always known at the British embassies in countries visited. At the end of an enjoyable evening he offered to run me back to the hotel in his car. I declined, wishing to save him the inconvenience, saying I was perfectly happy to go back in a bus, if there was one.

The bus provided an amusing interlude with a few local peasants returning from the country with a crate of live hens! My landmark was the huge PAN AM illuminated sign clearly visible on the roof of the hotel. On leaving the bus, I started to walk along a major thoroughfare towards the PAN AM sign. Almost immediately, the illuminated sign went out as did every other light in the vicinity.

I felt a strange wobble as everyone around me started running in all directions. The doors of a cinema nearby burst open disgorging a great many people in a state of panic. There had been an earthquake but I had not become aware of it until some minutes had elapsed and superficial damage to buildings became evident. The traffic lights having failed, there was chaos on the highway with much blowing of horns. The last half hour of near daylight had passed. It was quite dark, and I was lost!

Pausing for a moment to remember the direction in which I had last seen the PAN AM sign, I decided to walk on and to gradually bear right-handed in concentric circles, as it were, in the hope of finding the hotel. The streets were full of people frightened to remain in their dwellings. Parked cars had born the brunt of falling masonry. Families were huddled together on the pavements, where wooden fencing had been torn up and set alight to provide heat on a very cold night. Not surprisingly, no one was very interested in my predicament but I continued to mention the name of the hotel at every opportunity.

Eventually, and after an hour or so, I felt a bit desperate, separated from my belongings and lost in a strange city and with no means of communicating with those around me. In a quite extraordinary coincidence, I turned round to find myself standing outside the entrance to the hotel! The tactic of walking in circles had worked. I was amazed and hugely relieved.

Once inside the hotel, I found the extensive glass roof over the reception area a shattered mess on the floor. The walls were lined with people seeming to shelter from the risk of more material falling to the floor. Most of them had a drink in hand and that seemed a good idea. I made my way to a bar and paid the equivalent of a fiver for a glass of scotch. On the other side of the very crowded lounge, I spied a gentleman in a smart suit. His appearance and that of the suit seemed very English.

On introducing myself, he welcomed my company, explaining that he was a commercial traveller in machine tools and had found himself trapped in his room unable to open the door that had become jammed. We chatted about the incident against a background of many radios reporting the situations in various places. It was a mad house of excitement and emotion, as the extent of the effects of the earthquake became known. The epicentre was at Valparaiso just 50 miles to the north, where there was much loss of life and structural damage.

By and by, I went up to my room and found it much as I had left it. Bed seemed a sensible option, bearing in mind that I would be flying out to Punta Arenas in the morning – or would I, I asked myself.

The morning came all too soon – no water, no electricity and no breakfast. On checking out, I requested a taxi and was surprised that one was available. Off I went to Santiago airport, with the taxi driver skillfully negotiating the debris of buildings along the road and bringing me up to date with the situation.

I found the aircraft ready with a machine pumping warm air into the interior. I remember that as it was a cold, cold morning. But there was no heating or lighting in the airport, and worst of all no breakfast. A few passengers having arrived were concentrated on the daily paper. I found one, and although unfamiliar with the language, I could see from the photographs that there had been something of a national disaster. Having devoured a few chocolate bars and checked in, we took off for Punta Arenas.

Baggage at Punta Arenas was lying in rows out of reach behind a long barrier. Other passengers were pointing to their cases and receiving them from busy porters over the barrier. However much I pointed, my claim was ignored. It then dawned on me that all of the fingers enjoying success carried a tip! So, having extracted a 20 escudos bill from my wallet I got my bags.

On arriving at the hotel, surprise, surprise, my escort was relaxing in a chair awaiting my arrival. Following tea, we made plans for the evening at a very special restaurant. The dinner was absolutely superb.

The next day, an appointment had been arranged, namely to meet a Lt Col commanding an Alpine Regiment based outside the town. On arrival, at the entrance to the barracks, our credentials were checked by a most ferocious looking NCO, while two armed guards looked on. Following a very warm welcome from Col Georgios (forgotten his last name), we settled down to coffee and a chat with my escort as interpreter.

By and by, it transpired that an inspection of the troops by yours truly would be appreciated! They were formed up on the parade ground in four companies with their complete personal kit laid out for inspection. All these chaps were conscripts doing eighteen months national service and about to go on exercise high in the Andes, where they would live off the land.

Having dealt with the parade we retired to the Mess for lunch. It was a cold day, so much so that we all sat down to lunch in our great coats, there being no heating of any kind in the building.

With Colonel Jorge and his adjutant.

In the area, they had accommodated a club for the British ex-pat population during a period, long since gone, when the area attracted a great many sheep farmers from England. Over the entrance was a Coat of Arms with the words, Victoria Regina, all in stone. Peering through the windows, we could see the furniture covered with dust sheets and the billiard table similarly protected. An elderly local gentleman had come to tell us about the club and what went on there many years ago. He said there were still three members, a chairman, a secretary, and a treasurer, all relatives of former members who felt an obligation to maintain this historical building.

That evening, I was introduced to another excellent restaurant, where the two of us dined into the night while discussing the job I had to do next day amongst other topics. For the recce, we were met after breakfast by two Chilean Army subalterns.

Having studied their map and located the place where I needed to go, we set off in their transport. The site for satellite observations was on a farm. The intention was to set up the antenna on the top of a water tower thus achieving maximum observation from horizon to horizon.

The water tank was some 30 feet above ground level. To reach the roof of the tank it was necessary to climb a metal ladder. I was never very comfortable about heights but with members of the Chilean Army watching my progress, I had little option but to get up that ladder!

On reaching the top I made my notes, measured the angles to various features that might obstruct observations, took a deep breath, and very cautiously descended the ladder! Job done.

Discussing next location.

The water tower Harry had to climb.

The three of us returned to the town for lunch and a most enjoyable discourse over a fair amount of wine. That evening we returned to the restaurant we had visited on the first night and were made exceptionally welcome.

Very early the next morning we drove down to the water at Punta Arenas

With my escort.

to witness a most remarkable event, the arrival of a great many small boats loaded with supplies and provisions such as one would see at a market. These boats had come from the islands that form the western extremity of the southern end of Chile. A glance at the map shows literally hundreds of islands, populated by people producing all sorts of fruit and vegetables brought daily to Punta Arenas for sale. It was a magical experience to see all this in the early hours of the morning. The goods were displayed on the decks of the boats with whole families in attendance. The colours of the goods, the clothing and everything in sight were exotic.

Later the same day, I departed by bus for the journey to the Tierra del Fuego, leaving my escort to make his way back to Santiago. I did wonder why he had come all that way, but his company was welcome and I did need some guidance in such a strange area. In retrospect, I concluded that the Chilean authorities would not have been all that happy having a British Army officer roaming loose in the country!

The first part of the journey to the Tierra del Fuego was in an ancient bus in the company of a number of locals. After an hour and a half rattling along a bumpy and rutted road, we stopped for refreshments at a sort of café. Amongst the variety of things to eat, the only item I recognized was 'Kit-Kat'! So I bought half a dozen bars to keep me going until the uncertain end of the trip.

After another couple of hours, we reached the water, whereupon the few remaining passengers left the bus and made their way towards a vessel I can best describe as a World War II landing craft. As I could see the land to which we would be heading, the absence of any sort of shelter other than the sides of the open cargo space, was of no concern.

Crossing the Megallan Strait to Cape Horn.

By and by, engines started up, and with a grating noise the landing craft scraped its way off the gravel, turned and went out to sea. We thundered along at a good pace despite the obstruction to progress presented by the vessel's ramp. This form of transport following the three hour ancient bus trip suggested to me that I really was in the back of beyond! In due course, we bumped up onto the gravel on the other side and, praises be, there was my Captain RE standing by the ramp.

We retired to his quarters not far away in a nissen hut shared half-in-half by equipment. I was immediately aware that the site was one of the most basic and inhospitable places I'd visited so far.

After a couple of days, and the opportunity of watching the team at work during the transit of the satellite, I bade them farewell and made my way back to the landing craft for the return journey to Punta Arenas, and hence by air to Santiago, where I was re-united with my escort.

The next station to be occupied was at Arica, north and adjacent the border with Peru. Before going there, I was briefed about the state of the geodetic control for mapping of Chile at the headquarters of the Instituto Geographico Militar.

It became apparent that a considerable time had elapsed since the geodetic survey had taken place and that the accuracy of parts of it was suspect. This was attributed to inherent weaknesses due to the linear nature of the survey, Chile being a very long, narrow country. Furthermore, severe differences of elevations between the coast on the west and the mountainous Andes on the east had probably adversely affected the accuracy of observations using traditional methods: With a length of nearly 2800 miles, a width varying from only 100 to 50 miles and a difference in height between sea level at the coast and the pinnacles of the Andes in excess of 10,000 feet there existed a probability of some divergence dependent on astronomical observations.

With time on hands during the routine observation of satellite passes, there was opportunity to employ satellite survey techniques and verify the position of suspect control points to an accuracy that could not previously have been achieved. The verification and revision of control data was completed in a matter of a few weeks, whereas the Chilean authorities reckoned the work commissioned by themselves using triangulation and astronomy would have taken years.

My departure from Santiago Airport was unusual in so far as I quite unexpectedly found the General commanding the Instituto Geographico Militar, a few of his staff with whom I had been working, and the Chilian Army Captain who had so efficiently managed my programme present to see me off. The General presented me with a framed plaque. While the Instituto officers were chatting, the Captain popped a small package into my great coat pocket, and at the same time, he whispered that I need not be concerned but stressed that I should not attempt to open it until I was in the air.

After warm handshakes all round, I slipped through the gate and was off. Once airborne, I opened the package and found all the dollar bills which my escort had exchanged for escudos during my time in Chile, with a note requesting that I lodge the money in his account at the Dupont Circle Branch of the National Bank in Washington! Well, well, I thought, and remembered seeing a very prominent notice in large letters in the departure area of the airport indicating that it was a criminal offence to take Chilian currency out of the country! I was glad to have been in uniform and in the company of such distinguished people also in uniform while saying my goodbye.

In due course, the programme at Arica was completed and the team returned to Washington DC.

Shemya, Aleutian Chain – Alaska

The next mission worthy of mention was the operation that took place on the island of Shemya, a tiny island at the west end of the Aleutian Chain, stretching from Alaska across the Pacific towards Russia. Getting there to visit the team on the island was a most memorable journey, starting from the National Airport in Washington DC, with various stops along the way, arriving in Anchorage, Alaska.

I can't recall the name of the airline that took me to Shemya, but it was very small scale: Just two English Electra aircraft, both flown by the sons of the owner, a 75-year-old who having crashed a Pan Am aircraft somewhere in

The team's base at Shemya, Alaska.

South America in the 1930s had been sacked. He told me he had come north to Alaska with 25 cents and started his own show. By the way, the stewardess on my flight, where I was the only passenger, was his daughter – quite a family enterprise.

We took off from Anchorage and before long were flying at no great height over the islands forming the Aleutian Chain. Although stark white in all directions, it was a remarkable experience, appreciating the nature of that part of the northern territories. At times, we flew lower than the surrounding peaks and occasionally descended as if dive bombing a remote settlement. I was asked not to mention to Father the extent to which the quite large machine with four engines was being put through its paces!

On reaching Shemya, we made about six approaches flying low over the single runway, I assumed in order to get the landing right. On leaving the aircraft, the snow and ice on either side of the runway appeared to be higher than the aircraft, hence the need to make several approaches. The terminal building, if you could call it that, was a portakabin painted yellow and bearing the following information "Shemya – Males 9, females 0".

Adjacent was a larger more permanent building. Once inside, we sat down to a hearty fry-up meal, washed down with beer. It transpired that the runway was not short of a mile long and a strategic facility of international status with all sorts coming and going. By and by, I was introduced to a couple of young men who proudly described themselves as Aleuts, educated on the mainland, graduated from university and very good company. They took me off to meet the team and settle in at the accommodation.

During my visit to Shemya.

The next day, in a blizzard, I visited the team's location, remote from the accommodation to facilitate satellite observations. It was a nissen hut, almost buried in snow but very well appointed with creature comforts for interrogation of the satellite at any appointed hour of the day or night. I noticed a rifle on hand, considered necessary in the event of engaging some marauding predator, e.g. a bear!

I enjoyed the company of the two Aleutian chaps. They took me off to meet some locals found living in fairly basic huts, mostly corrugated tin. They were very welcoming, especially the children wrapped up in fur lined fleeces with head gear and muckluks (fur-lined Wellington boots). They had such chubby red cheeks. Talking to these people who had never left Shemya, nor known anything other than snow and ice made me think about their extraordinary life-style. There was an American PX (a small sort of Tesco market) on the island and I was glad to hear that the locals enjoyed access for provisions. Without that, it seemed that they would have to rely on hunting with sledge and dogs. Before leaving the island, I bought myself a pair of muckluks!

The return trip to Anchorage was interrupted by an emergency involving a woman in labour and needing treatment in hospital. She had been moved by boat to the nearest airfield. We landed at the appropriate location, and after a brief stop, set off with the patient who was greatly relieved to be on her way to hospital. The airline was a vital form of transport 'on call' for all sorts of reasons.

I stayed overnight in Anchorage, setting off for home in various stages with different national airlines flying south along the west coast of the continent. On arriving at Los Angeles, I remembered the Hannah family: neighbours years previously in Belfast when I was about ten or so years of age. David and Sheelagh Hannah had been playmates. Their parents Douglas and Fedelia Hannah had been great friends of my parents. Douglas had an Irish Linen shop in Belfast, and after the war he moved with his wife, family, and linen business to San Diego, where Fedelia's father had been Mayor.

I popped into a phone box at the airport and phoned the Hannah's number, one of a few in my diary given to me by Ma Crawford on the off-chance that I might make contact. Douglas Hannah answered the call. I said it's Harry Crawford, remember me? It was nearly thirty years since he had last seen me! After a short pause, during which the elderly Douglas recognized who was calling, he said slowly, with some emphasis, 'H a r r y C r a w f o r d, where are you?' I said I was in LA, on my way home to Washington DC. He said to get on the next plane for San Diego and that he would meet me at the airport.

That I did, and after about fifty minutes emerged at 'Arrivals' to see a white-haired Douglas with arms outstretched to embrace me. It was an emotional moment for both of us: total surprise for him and enormous pleasure for me on managing to make the contact.

On reaching his gorgeous home overlooking the harbour, I was warmly greeted by Fedelia, insisting that I would stay with them for a couple of days, at least. That same evening they had a dinner engagement with a neighbour and his wife. He was a US Navy Admiral, no less, and I was assured of a warm welcome for dinner.

At the conclusion of the meal the Admiral enquired what I might be doing next day. I had no plans and looked to Douglas for a response. Before Douglas spoke, the Admiral suggested we both accompany him on board an aircraft carrier for some trials to which he was committed. Douglas and I accepted with enthusiasm and rose early next morning to join our host for the drive to the Naval Base. I wore my uniform while Douglas wore his blazer with a Royal Artillery badge on the breast pocket and an RA tie. We had the most wonderful time during the day, as seemingly important guests being shown over the ship and spending quite a long time on the bridge.

The following day, Douglas took me on a tour of San Diego, and I was delighted to entertain Fedelia and him to dinner in the city. On the following morning, I returned to LA and took a flight direct to National Airport in Washington DC.

Thule, Greenland

Thule lies on the northwest coast of Greenland and is the home of Peterson Air Force Base, the US Air Force's most northernly base, 750 miles north of the Arctic Circle and just 947 miles from the north Pole. One-Hundred-and-forty airmen, along with 500 Danish and Greenlandic contractors, manned the base. The mission was two-fold: providing a Missile Early Warning System watching for ballistic missiles launched from the Russian landmass (like Fylingdales, North Yorkshire) and tracking satellites and orbiting debris. It was March, 1972, and cold, with night temperatures as low as -47 degrees.

With the Admiral commanding the US Coast Survey.

Some time later, and prior to a visit by my UK Boss, Brigadier Arthur Walmesley-White, the Admiral commanding the US Coast Geodetic Survey, for whom the team at Thule was working, suggested that he, one of his officers and my Boss should accompany me to Thule.

The arrangements were made by the Coast Survey staff, including a flight on a large Boeing passenger aircraft in which just the four of us were passengers. During the flight from Andrew's Air Force Base, I recall wandering back to the loo, and on emerging, that the long sausage shaped cabin was twisting ever so slightly in an extraordinary manner! The front end was twisting to the left and the part away at the back in which I was standing was twisting to the right. I suppose the curtains normally separating First and Economy class areas would make that less apparent.

Perhaps a full payload would also affect the movement.

On arriving at the Thule base, we weren't allowed to disembark until the aircraft was inside a huge hanger with the doors shut, such was the temperature outside. The Lieutenant Commander US Navy and I were accommodated in the same room within an accommodation block. The ceiling in the room was supported with steel 'I' beams, both vertically and horizontally. We were to learn that this was necessary on account of the severe wind that occurred during what was called a Storm Condition Delta.

During our briefing the precautions taken in connection with the storm condition were explained and the dangers of venturing outside inadequately clad at any time. We were introduced to the club which provided food, refreshments, leisure areas and warm shelter 24/7.

Thule is a remarkable place and on account of the time of year, March 1972, daylight was almost continuous. A few months previously, the Base would have been permanently dark and permanently very cold. Eighty percent of Greenland is ice more than a mile deep, creating a condition known as permafrost. The strong sunlight had an alarming effect on the terrain: buildings were insulated from the ground, lest the heat generated within them would melt the permafrost. The roads around the base waved up and down, such was the effect of the sun. Before leaving Washington, I had introduced my UK Boss to my American Boss, General Podufaly, the Commander of US Army Topographic Command. The General remarked to Arthur W-W to make sure they were still painting the 2-mile long runway white. We thought this was a bit of a joke but it was nothing of the sort. The runway was indeed painted white to deflect the rays of the sun and prevent the adverse effect on the permafrost. It was an ongoing procedure, not unlike the continuous painting of the Forth Railway Bridge.

One day during our visit, the public address system (speakers in every room on the base) announced that storm was forecast and that all personnel should move to the location at which duties might require them to be during the next couple of hours. For my colleague and I, the decision was obvious. We donned our winter clothing and made for the club.

The wind appeared to be increasing from dead calm to a steady breeze, with snow blowing all over the place. The public address system spluttered again, announcing that a severe storm was now imminent and that personnel needing to move should do so immediately or be prepared to remain where they were. We were happy in the club with a couple of tots of Jack Daniels. Shortly afterwards, visibility through the windows was obliterated with thick snow being blown with great intensity by the howling wind which had increased in velocity. A final announcement was heard to the effect that it was an offence for anyone to venture outside from their present location. The storm had arrived. We then heard that the wind was blowing at 207 mph causing havoc outside. We learned also that a party of men who had not moved when advised to do so were marooned in a building of relatively fragile construction such that they were in danger. They were rescued in Snowcat tracked vehicles.

Brigadier Walmesley-White with Captain Irwin.

The storm gradually blew itself out. It had been something of a rare experience for all concerned because storms of condition Delta were infrequent.

On a bright sunny morning we were escorted across the ice to a miniature iceberg protruding the surface to a height of about fifteen feet. Arthur W-W was invited to break off a small piece of ice. He took it back to the club and popped it into a G&T where upon the drink 'exploded'! This was apparently due to the age of the ice and was a prank played on most visitors.

We returned to Washington in one of those huge C17 aircraft fitted with para-jump seats along the sides of the vast interior. For a journey of several

A very old piece of ice at Thule US Air force Base.

The visitors at Thule Air Force Base.

hours, this was a bit uncomfortable and certainly not a normal arrangement for a Brigadier and an Admiral!

Brownsville, Texas

Compared with the other stations manned by my various teams, Brownsville offered a few luxuries but, oh boy, was it hot! The team on the job had previously been at Shemya, Alaska, so they found things at Brownsville altogether more satisfactory!

With the team at Brownsville, Texas.

Denver, Colorado

I was asked to visit a US Army Topographic Command station at Denver, to attend a reception, and to sign an agreement on behalf of the UK concerning the exchange of intelligence information between the UK and the USA. I stayed in the most comfortable Thomas Jefferson Hotel.

When sorting out my uniform for the special occasion I found to my horror that I had forgotten to pack my khaki tie. I confronted the bell hop with my problem, hoping that he might produce something similar. He queried the expression 'khaki', which we interpreted as light brown. He said upstairs there was a room full of clothing of all sorts including a great many ties. Away he went.

On his return, the few ties he had brought to me could not in any way be worn with my service dress. But he had an idea. All US army officers wear black ties so why don't you follow suit and wear a black tie tomorrow – Who's to know that you should be wearing the whatever-you-called-it tie. He produced a black tie which was worn next day, and I don't think anyone noticed it.

As happens on these occasions, photographs of the signing were taken and prints were circulated to all concerned, including Brigadier Walmsley-White at home. A short time later, I received one of his letters in a package, enclosing a khaki tie which, he thought, I might find useful!

In addition to commanding 512 Specialist Team RE, a second and in some ways my more important role, was personal representative of the Director of Military Survey UK in the USA. I enjoyed direct access to the General commanding US Army Topograph Command in Washington, to the Commander of ACIC, the Aeronautical Charting and Information Centre at St Louis, Missouri, to the Chief of the US Mapping and Aeronautical Charting Department at the Defense Intelligence Agency in the Pentagon, and to the Head of US Coast Geodetic Survey and Maritime Charting organisation in Maryland.

Brigadier Walmesley-White, UK Director of Mapping.

Those people and their huge organisations managed the land survey, aeronautical charting, and naval charting activities plus the intelligence collecting operations on which their products depended for information worldwide.

My job was to promote mutual co-operation between the UK and the USA in each of the agencies mentioned above. An additional objective was to establish my position as Assistant Director Survey in the USA, and there lay a difficulty. My predecessor had commanded 512 SPECTRE and had made it his business to liaise, from time to time, with the other agencies. Prior to my arrival that liaison was undertaken more formally by a UK civilian representing the intelligence department of the UK Military Survey organization at Feltham, London.

In order to establish the position of Assistant Director Survey UK in the USA, I was asked to create a single UK organisation comprising Personal Representative of Director of Military Survey, Commanding Officer 512 SPECTRE and an Intelligence gathering cell managed by the civilian officer. The difficulty was the opposition of the civilian officer to any notion of losing his independence and becoming part of the proposed single UK organization in the USA. To make matters worse, his boss in the UK supported the opposition, which the Director, Brigadier Walmesley-White, his superior, seemed unprepared to resolve.

It was left to me to force the issue and doing so generated a great deal of disharmony leading to a ridiculous situation with two UK people at loggerheads in Washington, while their superiors at home were not prepared to reach agreement and issue a directive for the reorganisation.

The civilian officer sought support from the Military Attache at the Embassy, claiming that Crawford was interfering with his work by seeming to duplicate his role in the business of collecting intelligence. I was summoned to the Embassy, where it was suggested that I had a personality problem! On explaining what I was trying to do on behalf of the Director UK, indeed as required by the Director UK, the response was to the effect that the Director should sort out his plans at home rather than present difficulties in Washington. I couldn't have agreed more but was not in a position to say so. I found it deeply embarrassing to be told by the Attache to lay off the civilian officer who had clearly won the argument.

The solution was found at TOPOCOM and at the Defense Intelligence Agency (DIA) in the Pentagon. I got on exceptionally well with the General in command of TOPOCOM and with the Head of DIA, so much so that having spilt the beans of the problem, I received a sympathetic response from both of those senior officers. The Director UK knew both of them well and they were keen to assist the implementation of the single organisation, which made sense to them. The General instructed his subordinate responsible for the allocation of office accommodation at TOPOCOM to require that the civilian's office be vacated and that he be relocated in the office occupied by myself.

The relocation took place just one week prior to the conclusion of my tour of duty in Washington, which was fortunate for both of us, there being little possibility of the disagreement perpetuated over three years being amicably resolved and a satisfactory working relationship achieved. Why the Director of Military Survey (UK) didn't over-rule his subordinate at home and issue a directive for the implementation of the change, I shall never know.

This unseemly situation was to adversely affect my position at the conclusion of my tour of duty. On saying goodbye to the Military Attache, he suggested that I should tell the UK Director of Military Survey to conduct his experiments elsewhere than in the United States.

In retrospect, I should have involved the senior staff at the Embassy in what I was doing. Why I didn't include the Attache on the circulation list for SPECTRE I shall never know. Doing so might have conveyed a better understanding of my role and that of my team. But informing embassy people was a problem, namely that no one, not even the Attache, enjoyed the high security clearance applicable at the time to intelligence collecting activities about which I was aware, and in which I had a responsibility for reporting results back to the UK.

I was held in high regard by all of the Americans with whom I was working at all levels, and this was made evident when I was recommended for The United States Legion of Honor. Unfortunately, the award had to be declined because such awards recommended by other nations cannot be accepted by British military personnel except in time of hostilities. The recommendation notified to me by the Director UK was, however, included in my records. Alas, my annual report was not written by the Americans.

US Army Topographic Command (TOPOCOM) was formed on 1 September 1968. On 1 July 1972, a reorganisation took place, namely the formation of the Defense Mapping Agency. I felt priviledged on receiving an invitation to attend the celebration of our past association, UK Military Survey and US Topocom, at a formal Dining-In held at the Fort Belvoir Officers' Club on 14 June 1972. During the dinner I presented the Commander, Colonel Anderson, with a framed map of Scotland, that part of the UK being associated with his family name. It was an unusual occasion with a US Army colour party parading the Stars and Stripes, side by side with the Union Jack, at the conclusion of the dinner. When, if ever, had the Union Jack been paraded by a US Army soldier?

Pa and Ma Crawford visited us in Washington by way of a holiday. I had mentioned their visit to General Podufaly, one of the US officers for whom I was working. During a reception he enquired about the circumstances in which Pa's Bronze Star had been awarded. The next day, the General extended an invitation to Pa to come to a briefing on the Apollo mission to the moon, which was then in progress.

On the appointed day, a staff car came to collect Pa for his briefing and lunch at the headquarters, where he met a number of US Army engineers and among them a General Gray, who had been invited from retirement to join the party.

General Gray didn't recognise Pa, but Pa certainly remembered him as he

```
DEPARTMENT OF THE ARMY
U.S. ARMY TOPOGRAPHIC COMMAND, CORPS OF ENGINEERS
            ARMY TOPOGRAPHIC STATION
              WASHINGTON, D.C. 20315
```

TPCCO(90000)   31 May 1972

LT COL H. G. W. Crawford, RE
Office of UK AD Survey (90140)
6500 Brooks Lane
U. S. Army Topographic Command
Washington, D. C. 20315

Dear Colonel Crawford:

In the past three decades, the military topographic community has developed into a forward thinking, highly professional and closely knit Corps. All of us can be proud of our contributions to establishing topographic organizations which respond effectively and aggressively in providing a wide variety of standard and special topographic products. Now, our topographic community routinely provides outstanding support to the Army.

One milestone in the development of the current military topographic capability was formation of the United States Army Topographic Command (TOPOCOM) on 1 September 1968. As a key element of TOPOCOM, your organization can be justifiably proud of your contribution.

It is appropriate that we celebrate our past association before the organizational changes occasioned by the formation of the Defense Mapping Agency become effective on 1 July 1972. Traditionally, the formal Dining-In is a ceremonial evening reserved for special occasions where officers meet in a spirit of comradeship to celebrate an event of particular significance. Accordingly, I have scheduled the last formal Dining-In of TOPOCOM to celebrate our long and rewarding relationship.

All of the officers of your command are invited to attend the formal Dining-In to be held at the Fort Belvoir Officers' Club on 14 June 1972.

                                    Sincerely,

                                    E. G. ANDERSON, JR.
                                    Colonel, Corps of Engineers
                                    Commanding

The invitation to celebrate the formation of the US Defense Mapping Agency.

The dinner at Fort Belvoir.

Presenting a map of Scotland to Colonel Anderson.

Presenting a 512 Spectre plaque to Colonel Anderson.

With the guard of honour at the dinner.

was the senior American who had recommended Pa for the Bronze Star during the campaign in Italy. The occasion was, needless to say, a highlight of the holiday visit. I had to be away in Canada that day and much regretted not being able to listen to the pair of them reminiscing about the Salerno landings, the incident on the Volturno River, among other shared experiences and memories.

My departure from the USA was punctuated with a series of farewell parties at which I found just about everyone I had known and worked with during the three-year tour of duty. On arriving at Dulles Airport for my RAF flight home, I was more than a little surprised to find a representative crowd of people I had known particularly well to see me off.

The tour of duty in the United states should have been a stepping stone to promotion. Instead, it was marred by the problems already mentioned and for two other reasons: the weakness of the Director of Military Survey, Arthur Walmsley-White, who seemed to ignore the re-organisation matter, failed to recognise the successes achieved on behalf of the UK and felt unable to support me. He was the only Director who didn't make Major-General, and it was my bad luck that my tour of duty in the States coincided with his own tour of duty at the head of Military Survey. I had served previously with two of his predecessors and wished so very much that either of them had been in charge while I was serving in the States: neither of them would have tolerated the dispute over the re-organisation.

The other reason was personal, namely that my marriage was on the rocks, leading to inevitable divorce. I need to explain why my marriage had failed but must recognise that my wife was adored by our two adopted daughters, and since they will read this explanation, it must seem to be reasoned and free from spite. I read somewhere that if marriage isn't the women's career, it won't be a good marriage. That will seem chauvinistic, unless the expression is considered in terms of loyalty, loyalty to the man's career. Ronald Reagan's wife, Nancy, devoted her life to her husband's political career. She advised on White House hirings and firings and dictated his timetable; what a girl!

People I have known during my military service who have achieved senior rank have without exception enjoyed the support of their wives. By 'support' I mean a sort of dedication that perhaps doesn't apply in any other profession. I didn't enjoy that support. My wife's primary interests were family, her relatives and our own family. My career was something subordinate to those interests, something that wasn't thought about very much. I remember at the time of our engagement being warned by her grandmother that managing money was not her forte. She was a compulsive spender, and it was not until I provided her with her own bank account in the States that I recognised that problem. Time and time again, I had to deal with her excessive spending, which was a drain on our resources.

The real crunch came when I was denied the privilege, indeed the honour, of giving away our eldest daughter on the occasion of her marriage. This shocking decision aided and abetted by my mother-in-law was delegated to my wife's step-father, a person for whom I had little respect. He had been a friend of my wife's family during the war years and had married my widowed mother-in-law while we were in the States. He had not been involved with the children's upbringing and consequently had no right whatsoever to control the arrangements for the wedding. I never forgave my wife for having agreed to such a deplorable decision.

– 18 –
Headquaters Ordnance Survey
Southampton

My next appointment on returning to the UK was Assistant Director Topography at the HQ in Southampton – a second tour with the ordnance Survey of Great Britain. There were six Regional Officers for England, Wales, and Scotland, namely SWRO (South West), SERO (South East), EMRO (East Midlands), WRO (West Midlands), NORO (North), and SCOTRO (Scotland), the latter being the appointment I had enjoyed previously.

Having been a Regional Officer, the role and responsibilities of ROs were well known to me. My new job entailed co-ordinating the activities of the ROs, responding to issues raised by them, and making liaison visits to their areas of responsibility.

An ROs conference was held annually at the HQ under the chairmanship of the Deputy Director Field Survey (DDFS). The conference provided an opportunity for the ROs to raise concerns and suggestions and for DDFS to present new policy and new arrangements concerning field survey activities. The discussions and debate that took place were interesting.

I much enjoyed sailing with Robin Gardiner-Hill who owned a fine yacht built in timber in Danzig, named *Pentina* and kept on a mooring at Buckler's Hard in Southampton Water. For several years at Easter, we sailed overnight to Cherbourg, arriving around 6.00 a.m to tuck into a breakfast of oysters and ice-cold muscadet. There was usually a good number of UK yachts in the harbour and socialising from one to another was most entertaining. On one occasion, we were due back at work on a Tuesday morning which meant departing on Sunday, in spite of an unfavourable weather forecast. Crossing the Channel was uneventful, but on arrival off the Isle of Wight early on Monday morning, we encountered a Force 6 and a tide which prevented us reaching Southampton Water. We tacked for several hours but made no headway until the storm and the sea abated. A lot of coffee laced with rum was consumed, but it was impossible to attempt cooking breakfast.

My work as AD Topo was most enjoyable. It was during my time at Southampton that I heard that my next appointment would be Commandant, Royal School of Military Survey at Hermitage in Berkshire. Towards the end of my three year tour in the Ordnance Survey, I gave notice of my intention to resign and did so in March 1976. Since I was then in a relationship with my future wife, dealing with divorce while at Hermitage was unthinkable.

– 19 –
Retirement from the Army

When I retired from the Army, there was an opportunity to attend a Resettlement Board to discuss preferences for employment with all sorts of employers with a registered interest in ex-service personnel. Having selected a preferred occupation, an introduction to the employer was arranged. In retrospect, I didn't give enough thought to that process and hastily opted for an interview at the Southampton Branch of the Sun life Insurance Company of Canada with little knowledge of the employment that might be offered. Another mistake. I should have requested an interview with British Railways, where I subsequently discovered retired Lieutenant-Colonels Royal Engineers were frequently recruited.

As my father had been a civil engineer with the Great Northern Railway, Ireland, and had distinguished himself during World War II with the recovery of railways in Tunisia and Italy, and my grandfather had been Traffic Manager with the same railway, their connections would almost certainly have supported my appointment to a position with British Railways. I might then have had a secure salaried position, with regular working conditions, instead of having to rely on nebulous commissions with Sun Life of Canada and the necessity of being virtually self-employed.

As an attractive aside, British Railways employees and their spouses are awarded life-time free travel on the railway both in the United Kingdom and in Europe. So, my failure to explore employment with the railway was an instance of shocking bad judgement that had adverse implications for the rest of my working life and, indeed, beyond.

– 20 –
Sun Life Assurance Company of Canada

During an interview with the branch manager, I was offered a job selling insurance and investments, subject to passing a routine suitability assessment and succeeding with a period of training. The assessment took place there and then in the form of a questionnaire, which I was invited to complete. I could tell from the nature of the questions that my answers would or would not concur with the company's standards regarding character, politics, religion, aspirations, and so on. It was a routine procedure and I was pleased, when my responses had been checked, to find I was considered a suitable candidate. I was introduced to a section leader, who was to become a great friend. He had been a national service officer in an infantry battalion. The training programme was explained and a date on which I would start the course agreed

After a few months during which I became familiar with the company's products and the appropriate paperwork, application processes, etc., I was in at the deep end. Salary was in two parts: a fixed monthly rate, plus commission on sales. I quickly grasped the swing of things and with some success started winning awards, e.g. a set of eight sterling silver teaspoons with emblems at the top of each spoon, in a smart presentation case. This was the result of a good month of sales. It was encouraging.

Cold canvassing was permitted in my day, but that has been long since discontinued. I noted engagements for marriage in the local press, researched the addresses of the ladies concerned and sent them a single A4 page, setting out the attractions of life assurance and investment for the future. This was followed up with an evening telephone call, offering to explain selected products face to face. I kept records of these approaches and soon discovered that 50% of such approaches not only resulted in a sale, but in most cases established an interest that could be followed up later as the circumstances of the families developed, e.g births of children, house purchase, and protection with life assurance. By and by, that percentage increased. Additionally the office would send me referrals, e.g. enquiries from the company's continuous advertising campaign in the national and financial press, the names and addresses of clients with maturing policies, who could reasonably be visited. Such visits frequently resulted in a further sale.

During my second year in the job, and having received several awards, I was invited to join a party of successful people meeting at a hotel in Eastbourne, where there would be an opportunity to meet the president of the company on a visit from Canada. This turned out to be a lavish occasion, with a programme of addresses by company executives, opportunities to meet other employees, black tie dinners, and all in a most enjoyable and comfortable atmosphere. It lasted three days, and I felt privileged to have been invited to such an event.

Working for the Sun Life of Canada was certainly a means of earning a lot of money provided one recognized and exploited the opportunities, complied with the rules, and had a flair for winning the confidence of prospective clients. I enjoyed meeting clients, and in several instances, I would be approached by relatives and friends to whom my advice had been recommended. In all of these ways, the occupation proved successful. However, the evening being the best time to visit, and the time preferred by most contacts, I found myself leaving home just as my wife was arriving from her job as an Executive Officer (Humanities) Ministry of Defence. This was most unsatisfactory, and a lifestyle which neither of us considered acceptable. After much thought, we decided that I should resign.

Attending the dinner at the Eastbourne hotel.

– 21 –
Hosier Farming Systems Limited
Collingbourne Ducis

Hosier Farming Systems had its factory and offices in the Wiltshire village of Collingbourne Ducis, where we lived. While working for the Sun Life of Canada, I had been looking over my shoulder at the possibilities of having a job there. A vacancy for the post of Production Controller was advertised in the local rag, and I decided to apply.

The interview was conducted by the Managing Director who gave me the impression that he had been a disappointed National Service man. At one stage in the proceedings, he said, "You're officer class and wouldn't fit in here." He was a blunt and somewhat arrogant Yorkshire man. Nevertheless, he would think about my interest and let me know. During the following week, a letter arrived offering me the post.

The firm had been started by one Julias Hosier at the beginning of the century. By fitting agricultural equipment to the rear end of trucks and even cars, he had pioneered the introduction of mechanised farming in Wiltshire. But his most famous invention was the Hosier Bale – a milking parlour on wheels that could be moved around the fields of the farm. When I joined the firm, production was concentrated on milking parlours of a more static type and capable of accommodating twenty or more cows with a vacuum operated milking facility and a degree of automation.

Orders taken were designed in the drawing office, manufactured in the workshops, equipped with milking equipment, transported to site, and installed by fitters. My job was to co-ordinate the provision from order to delivery.

There had been a history of late deliveries, due to lack of co-ordination between the departments and a shortage of parts that delayed the completion of the product. Initial reaction to my attempts to plan the whole process, and notify to the customer a reliable delivery date, met with a good deal of opposition. My interference with the laissez-faire routine previously enjoyed by the departmental managers was resented. They objected to my seeming to interfere. By and by, however, and despite their tacit objections, I achieved a modicum of success.

Orders began to reach customers on time but, alas, frequently short of essential parts known as 'shortages'. Shortages were a major problem. It seemed impossible to manufacture parts at a rate consistent with demand, with the result that orders were delivered with items essential for the operation of the plant missing and marked 'To follow'. In an attempt to resolve the problem, I devised a record of the missing items with part number, order number, etc. It was then possible for the Workshops Manager to see at a glance where the priorities lay. The record didn't resolve the problem entirely because the production capacity of the workshops was limited. At least, however, the quantities of items short were known, whereas previously it was all very haphazard with the customers who could shout loudest getting attention.

On the occasion of daughter Sarah Watkins' confirmation, there was a hefty snow storm. Austin and Caroline Bendall had come down from London and were unable to drive home such was the depth of the snow. Conversation with Austin got round to my dissatisfaction with the out of date administrative procedures at Hosier. Being a Director at the Coopers & Lybrand firm of management consultants, he was interested. Austin explained how Hosier could apply to the Department of Trade and Industry for a survey of the procedures currently in force.

To make a long story short, I was able to persuade the directors to accept a survey by Messrs Cooper & Lybrand free of charge! During a period of two weeks, a couple of consultants investigated each work place in great detail. At the end a senior presented a glossy report to the Board of Directors with 31 recommendations, each of which would result in a significant saving of time and money. There was an opportunity to rid the system of laborious manuscript documentation, duplication of effort, the holding of obsolete parts in the stores, and an opportunity to introduce up to date procedures that would greatly improve efficiency.

The report was well received, and it was decided at that meeting that I should draw up a plan for the execution of the recommendations. Sadly, however, it became obvious to me that the resistance to change that was inherent at Hosier from top to bottom would prevent any possibility of progress. Twelve months later not one of the recommendations had been adopted. It was a classic case of old ways of doing things taking precedence over modern administrative systems, employed by small industrial firms up and down the country with far ranging benefits.

On another occasion, I got talking to a representative of the Westland Helicopter Company at Yeovilton. They were interested in the possibility of manufacturing microlight aircraft for third world agricultural enterprises, but preferred to sub-contract the work. After a good deal of discussion about the feasibility of manufacturing microlights at Hosier. I persuaded the directors to invite my contact for discussion.

The directors were impressed and agreed to allow engineers from Westland to visit the Hosier Workshops with a view to examining the compatibility of the skills, trades, plant, and machinery. Their report to my contact, and hence to the directors at Westland, concluded that Hosier could satisfy all of their requirements. Westland then proposed that two microlights be built by Hosier, under the supervision of Westland's engineers, and that one of them be shown and demonstrated in flight at the subsequent Royal Agricultural Show at Stoneleigh. Costings were prepared and the sum of £60,000 was offered by Westland. A Westland director met the Hosier board and, it seemed, the project could proceed. Alas, Hosier's Managing Director, a majority share-holder wedded to milk, over-ruled the initiative. I found this lack of vision and reluctance to diversify extremely disappointing.

A short time later, the government introduced milk quotas as a means of reducing the quantity of milk produced in the UK surplus to requirements. The effect of this on Hosier was catastrophic; farmers didn't need large milking parlours, nor the smart stainless steel bulk tanks built in Belgium and standing in the Hosier yard. Orders were cancelled and in rapid succession to such an extent that Hosier's order book was severely diminished.

There was a lot of money outstanding at this time due to unpaid invoices. During an overnight reorganisation, I found myself in a new role, namely Credit Controller. My brief was to tackle the outstanding accounts and reduce the indebtedness. The customers concerned were inclined to ignore requests, followed by demands for payment. Requests by telephone were useless. The 'cheque is in the post' response became common practice. It was seldom in the post.

I decided the only way to deal with the situation was to arrive on the farm and demand the money. Surprisingly this approach worked, and I frequently returned from a tour of South Wales with a fist full of cheques, the majority of which proved good on presentation. My tactics involved enjoying a tour of the farm, having tea and many varieties of fruit cake, discussing the difficulties in agriculture, etc., etc., but never mentioning the matter of an outstanding invoice. Eventually, the conversation ran dry, and the silence was happily broken by the customer saying "I think you want some money?" or words to that effect. The cheque was then written, and I went on my way.

During my time on the fringe of the Accounts Department, I discovered that my salary lagged considerably behind that enjoyed by my contemporaries. I had suspected this was the case for a long time, but the proof of it annoyed me. It was known, you see, that I had a substantial Army pension, which led to the assumption that I really didn't need a salary at all! When gentle and discreet suggestions for a review failed to attract attention, I decided enough was enough, got myself made redundant and jumped ship.

A year later Hosier Farming Systems went down the pan and was taken over by one of its competitors. As far as I was concerned, that writing had been on the wall for a very long time. A gradual decline had stemmed from the most appalling management imaginable, coupled with an acute resistance to the need for development and diversification. Hosier had been great in the past. Its reputation was unnecessarily destroyed by arrogance and incompetence.

– 22 –
Marlborough Downs Training Group
Marlborough

With not much to do, and with an eye on the local job market, I noticed a vacancy for a Group Training Officer in the Marlborough Downs area, advertised by the Agricultural Training Board (ATB). I applied and was interviewed by Robert Lawton, Group Chairman, and his committee, and offered the post the same evening. The job entailed visiting member farmers, discussing their training needs, and those of their workers and putting together a training programme to satisfy those needs. The ATB had a pool of instructors for all aspects of farming, e.g. field skills, veterinary, finance, management, and health and safety. All I had to do was produce the programme, book the instructors, arrange the venues, organise the training sessions, and manage the accounts. It wasn't very difficult and it afforded me an opportunity of learning a bit about farming. A particular advantage for me was being able to do the job as and when convenient.

There were some 35 members – all sorts, from wealthy landowners with farm managers to yeoman farmers, often working their smallholdings single-handedly. Having sorted my first programme I soon learnt that of, say, 10 applicants for a session only 2 or 3 turned up. This played havoc with the bank balance since the instructors had to be paid, and those who failed to attend were not all that keen to cough up. This was remedied by getting payments up front and by charging a little more than was needed in order to create a bank balance that would cope with the 'no shows'. After that, things settled down to an easily managed routine.

The annual AGM was a terrible bore, with the usual AGM type agenda held in a pub in near darkness, such was the state of the lighting, and, as happens with AGMs, poorly attended. To correct this state of affairs, I found a better venue, namely John Jones' Royal Oak pub at Wootton Rivers, where the AGM was followed by a dinner for members, their ladies, and guests. With an interesting guest speaker and a good menu, the house was full to capacity. In fact, it was difficult to close the occasion much before midnight. It became a great annual event when members who often had not met each other were able to have a welcome get-together.

Another benefit was the much improved attendance at the AGM when the debate threw up lots of new ideas. For instance, the need for sessions addressed by the agricultural representatives of the High Street banks. Lloyds, Barclays and the NatWest ran most interesting evenings for me, spelling out their lending policies and explaining how applications should be presented. On another occasion, a representative from the General Accident Insurance Company answered a wide range of questions on insurance. As a result of that, several members had their portfolios reviewed, out-of-date cover upgraded, obsolete cover cancelled, and so on. These meetings with the professionals proved extremely helpful.

During this time, I enjoyed a close working relationship with the chairman, Robert Lawton. He was an exceptionally successful businessman and a joy to work for. He was a big man in every way. After six years in the job, it was time to move on.

– 23 –
Wiltshire County Council
Trowbridge

One morning when collecting the newspaper, I bumped into my old friend Bertram Sample. "How would you like to become a County Councillor?" was his opening remark. "An election is coming up and, it has been said, the electorate is none too pleased with the incumbent representing the Collingbourne Division. You could stand for any of the political parties. Think about it."

My initial reaction was one of amazement that he or anyone else should think that I could fill that role. It was not something I would have considered in my wildest dreams. However, consider it I did, and we subsequently discussed the implications at length. Bertram was, of course, deep into local politics having been a District Councillor and Parish Councillor for a good many years. I was then a Parish Councillor and had served under his chairmanship, so I had an inkling of the workings of local government.

Having decided to have a go, Bertram volunteered to act as my agent and we set about planning a campaign that would get Crawford elected. The Division's electorate comprised some 4000 souls, the majority of whom would have to be visited on their doorsteps during the forthcoming five weeks. And there would have to be some visual promotion of the candidate, with a manifesto circulated far and wide. A photograph was duly taken, and a manifesto drafted in Liberal party colours, that being the party I had chosen to represent, had joined, and in which my candidature had been accepted by Jack Ainslie, the local chairman.

Bertram came up with the idea of displaying yellow boards some 6ft by 4ft bearing the words "Welcome to Crawford Country" in large black capitals. These were positioned at each of the accesses to the Divisional area,

Standing for election to Wiltshire County Council.

COLLINGBOURNE DIVISION
Wiltshire County Council Election

Vote CRAWFORD on Thursday, 2nd May

I BELIEVE

* THAT the Government's attempts to interfere with and limit local spending must be stopped.

* THAT the continual decline of rural facilities and amenities must be resisted – our shops, Post Offices and schools, to name a few.

* THAT our children must be given equal opportunities in education, their parents full and fair participation on closures and that schools must be judged in relation to the overall needs of communities – not in isolation.

* THAT facilities for adult education and recreation must be established for communities – not remote centres.

* THAT social services for health and welfare must preserve the dignity and independence of those whom they seek to help – the elderly, our pensioners and the so very young future generation.

* THAT the imposition on our environment caused by excessively large heavy vehicles frustrated, at times, by intense holiday traffic must be recognised, damage to our roads and pavements stopped and weight restrictions on minor roads imposed.

* THAT diversion, for instance to the A34, must be adopted as a substitute for high cost and locally ineffective by-pass schemes that fail to materialise; with a view to a dramatic improvement in road safety for all.

* THAT unemployment must be fought and prosperity restored by increasing economic activity in both urban and rural areas to encourage and support new commercial opportunities.

* THAT school leavers, newly weds and first-time home buyers must cease to feel helpless in a notion of impossibility brought about through no fault of their own.

* THAT PEOPLE MATTER MORE THAN PARTY POLITICS.

I BELIEVE .... DO YOU?

Let's hope that you do, that you will exploit my determination to succeed and prove it by voting

YOUR CANDIDATE

On my retirement from the Royal Engineers with senior honorary rank at age 48, my wife and I established a permanent home in Collingbourne Ducis.

Now 56 years old, with eight years of valuable commercial experience, I recognise that much needs to be done in our towns and villages – there are many problems and seemingly few remedies.

Having served on my Parish Council for the past three years I am ready to assert myself on behalf of all of the people in the pursuit of practical common-sense solutions vigorously represented at County Hall.

CRAWFORD

Your Liberal-SDP Alliance Candidate
on
Thursday, 2nd May, 1985

Sorry you were out when I called - Harry Crawford

My manifesto for the election.

with the permission of friendly landowners, and were readable by passing motorists. It was a brilliant idea. In a short space of time, the question "Who's Crawford?" was being asked all over the place! This coupled with my daily round of door-knocking gradually got the locality bored to death with the sight of the name Crawford. I assiduously followed my programme of visits here, there and everywhere, up hill and down dale until the date for the election became imminent. The boards were checked every morning, and as was expected, some found to have been removed. But we had a few in reserve. One in particular, I remember, had been amended to read "Crawford is Crap"!

Starting the week before the election, Bertram and the candidate myself toured the whole area in his Land Rover, with Bertram bellowing on the loud hailer "Vote for your LOCAL candidate" and a few other encouragements besides. The Labour candidate was not local and had done himself a great disservice by poking little notes in 2B pencil through too few letter boxes. The Conservative candidate was somewhat unfortunately called Copp and hadn't been seen anywhere. We therefore soldiered on blasting the whole place with confidence.

At last, the dawn of election day. That was something of a relief since candidates are not permitted to canvass on election day. Instead, we made our presence known by our large colourful rosettes at the various polling stations, accepting smiles of recognition from some and frowns of obnoxious displeasure from the opposition. One thing was for certain, the man Crawford was known. He had been met by a great many people and had been generally well received.

As the closing of the ballot boxes approached, Bertram, myself, and the family assembled for the count together with the other candidates in a stiffly silent atmosphere of apprehension. As the boxes of voting slips were turned out for counting by the team of busy bees and tied with elastic bands, before being placed in one or other of the three party trays, Bertram's glowering expression gradually took on the hint of a smile and eventually one of rapturous pleasure – his boy was winning!

At the end, we had achieved a clear majority of more than 2000 votes. I can't remember exactly how many. I was flabbergasted. Following a few words of condolence to the other candidates, about their well-fought campaign sort of stuff, and grateful thanks to my supporters, a large number of whom had arrived unnoticed by me, we retired home for a few drinks with delighted main-stream helpers.

That night, the Liberals took 25 seats in the County Council and was thus placed to run the administration for the next four years. While reflecting upon my majority which, incidently, was the highest of the 25, I came to realise that person-to-person canvassing had won the day.

I may have worn down a few pairs of shoes, but the real credit for the success went to Bertram who had managed me and the whole campaign with tremendous flair. I was grateful.

The next day, the phone was busy as the news of the election results hit the local headlines. Although my political sentiments in the past had been more conservative than anything else, I was quite glad to see the Liberal Party taking its place in local government in its own right, not only in Wiltshire, but elsewhere in the UK as well. And I felt privileged to have been able to contribute towards that result.

A particular telephone call from Jack Ainslie's right hand man, Byron Carron, came as a great surprise. Would I be prepared to take the chairmanship of the Transport and Highways Committee in the new administration? This I accepted but was very conscious of moving into uncharted waters.

The following day, the chairmen of the various committees were summoned to County Hall where their individual appointments were formally accepted. Immediately after that, the Chief Officers of the Council's departments arrived and mysteriously, I thought, found their new chairmen who were whisked away to meet the departmental subordinates.

The Chief Officer in my case was John Davies, a splendid fellow with whom I was to establish a remarkable working relationship such was our mutual understanding of the business in hand. That relationship became a friendship. I have corresponded with him at Christmas ever since. He invited me to the annual dinner of the Society of County Surveyors held in luxurious surroundings in London. At other times, we travelled together to many, many meetings in the South-West, and elsewhere, presenting the Wiltshire view on a whole range of transport topics.

Each year we attended a conference chaired by myself and attended by Peter Bottomley MP, who was Minister for Roads, in the Conservative government. On those occasions, money and our priorities for the attention of central government were high on the agenda. The members present representing all three parties and, of course, their own electorates wrestled for consideration of their particular objectives.

John Davies, sitting on my right, was able to whisper useful comments and guide me through the debate with reminders about this and that. One of the many solicitors sat on my left with responsibility for ensuring that I conducted the proceedings in accordance with the law. Reaching a consensus, the chairman's job, was sometimes tricky, steering the vote towards achieving the Department's aims and objectives for Wiltshire was frequently difficult. You won some and lost some, the losses usually for party political or selfish territorial reasons and not always in the best interests of the County as a whole.

I was not a political person as was widely recognised. My aim in all things was to obtain the most appropriate technical decision and, as far as was possible, to support the policies of the Department. I made a point of getting to know the 30 or so members of the committee, getting to know their particular hobby horses and seeking all the time to put across the bigger Wiltshire picture. I found that that sort of lobbying made things easier in committee. It smoothed rough edges during debate.

My non-political attitude and my informal chats with members, disregarding party politics, led to something of a crisis. Certain members of my own party objected to my seeming to wish to be all things to all men. There was also some criticism of my preparedness in committee to listen unduly to the representations of members, notably of the other parties. I ignored all that and continued to run my show as I best knew how. The result was a few enemies within never mind those without! At the same time, I was aware that a majority on all sides of the Council respected my ways. This led to a strange belief in some quarters that I was about to cross the floor, e.g. to join the Conservatives! It was my opinion that these criticisms and the innuendos that flashed from time to time reflected an element of competition for position rather than reasoned judgement. The situation was par for the course in politics, whether I liked it or not. After all, one sees it on political television every day of the week.

My greatest interest was the problem of traffic on the County's road network. With the M4 and the M3 motorways lying on an east-west axis, and with traffic from the south coast ports destined for the midlands along relatively minor routes, Wiltshire contained an unsatisfactory cross roads. Traffic moved east-west with ease, traffic moved north-south with difficulty on B numbered routes imposing much inconvenience, noise, hazard, and environmental disturbance in the many villages along those routes.

My opposite number in Dorset shared my concern which I had raised with Peter Bottomley during the annual conference. She was acutely aware of the problem due to the quantity of heavy goods traffic arriving from France at the ferry terminal at Poole, and vice versa, and moving north/south along unsuitable roads in Dorsetshire. We got together with our respective Chief Officers and agreed to concentrate resources on an improvement of the route from Poole north past Warminster and along the A46 to the midlands. A motorway was out of the question but a widening of the route, and the by-passing of the towns and villages, was a feasible objective over a period of time conditioned, of course, by funding. It was our view that the provision and promotion of a decent route would attract the HGV drivers who were otherwise using a variety of unsuitable routes, selected arbitrarily from Ordnance Survey maps.

The lady chairman in charge in Dorset had enjoyed some liaison with her opposite number in Cherbourg, through which the traffic in question was proceeding to and from Poole. In the course of our discussions, it became apparent that we might introduce the French connection with a view to bolstering our case for central government funding for our south to north scheme. She arranged for us together with our small staff of advisers to be invited to Cherbourg for a meeting with the President of the Cherbourg Region, equivalent to our County Councils.

We set sail one glorious morning on the Brittany Ferry for Cherbourg and were generously entertained to a splendid breakfast en route, taken up to the Bridge for a most interesting explanation of all that went on there with emphasis on a TV screen showing the bow doors. Quite unexpectedly, we were treated as VIPs, which we thought we were, but didn't appreciate that anyone else was aware of it!

We were met with smart cars when we disembarked at Cherbourg and zoomed off to the City Chambers to be met by the President, an enormous man with not a hair on his head. The welcome over coffee was as warm as could be.

What came next was quite a shattering experience. We were taken to the site of an unfinished motorway running from Spain to Cherbourg along which it was proposed to route all commercial traffic for Poole from Spain and the west coast of France destined for the UK. Imagine how we felt while watching that mammoth road building operation and thinking of the roads that would attempt to contain the traffic moving north from Poole. It seemed unbelievable that this was happening unknown to the UK government.

We retired to a sumptuous lunch in a rather special restaurant, where the wine poured freely. In the afternoon, I presented our appreciation of the situation in my best French reading from a text prepared for me by a lass in the home Council, with whom I had rehearsed the speech several times. The discussion that followed was conducted in English with our Poole Harbour Master fluent in French interpreting for the several French officials who had something to say. We then retired to our hotel as guests of the Cherbourg authority.

A few hours later we joined transport for a short trip to another restaurant where we sat down to a dinner of goodness how many courses in the company of two French MPs together with all of those met during the day. It was quite a party, and it went on well beyond midnight. I was presented with a splendid book entitled Et la liberte vint Cherbourg – La bataille logistique de la liberation". It is a remarkable account of the destruction of the city during the war, the subsequent siege and the liberation with hundreds of photographs and, of course, all in French! It's just one of the many treasures I have been privileged to receive during my varied occupations.

On returning home, I got John Davies to arrange for me to meet Peter Bottomley at the Department of Transport for as many minutes as he could spare. I went up to London on my own for what promised to be a ten-minute audience. After an hour and a nice tea, I reckoned he had received my concerns about the development in Cherbourg. Moreover, he offered to meet the lady from Dorset and our Chief Officers at County Hall, Wiltshire, to discuss the implications for the United Kingdom.

Following that meeting, the by-passing of Warminster was funded by central government, together with the widening of various sections of the preferred routes in Dorset and Wiltshire. It gave me great pleasure to invite Peter Bottomley to open the Warminster bypass on its completion and to return the hospitality enjoyed in Cherbourg with the President present.

The Wiltshire County Council ran with the efficiency of a sewing machine. The meetings of the full Council were good fun. We chairmen sat in the high altar either side of Jack Ainslie, Chairman of the Council. The Chief Officers sat around a table below, with the Press around another. The Conservative members sat in the stalls on the right, the Liberals in the centre with Labour on the left.

As the agenda was debated, questions inevitably arose and were addressed to the appropriate committee chairman for his or her response. The serious business was punctuated with a good deal of frivolity. The opposition would repudiate the responses at great length. Much of what was said by members was aimed for reporting by the Press, thus demonstrating to the electorate that their representatives were doing a good job! It was frequently necessary for me following a council meeting to shut myself in a studio to respond to questions on the telephone about the proceedings live on Wiltshire radio. Those radio interviews and many others conducted on the telephone, required caution in the knowledge that everything said would be heard or read in the next issue of the *Wiltshire Gazette*.

– 24 –
Hanover Housing Association
Wiltshire

When I was a member of Wiltshire County Council, remuneration amounted to valid expenses for motor mileage, hotel accommodation, and anything else in connection with expenses incurred while undertaking official duties and visits. Subsequently, local authority councilors were paid a salary plus expenses. As I didn't enjoy that income, I needed to find a job that would supplement my Army pension. I noticed an advertisement offering a position for a Housing manager with the Hanover Housing Association in the Andover area, applied for an interview, and was accepted. The Association provided retirement homes, with a round-the-clock response service in blocks of flats, apartments, and in bungalows for over-55-year-olds – 19,000 properties in 600 locations throughout the UK.

I became responsible for a block of properties in Andover, with responsibility for managing maintenance, prompt repairs, maintaining a positive dialogue with residents and the warden, motivating the warden, and generally working rather like a bursar at a school. An important advantage was being able to fit my work in with my County Council commitments. It was a very flexible job with no nine-to-five routine. It suited me very well, was enjoyable, and during the following twelve months my responsibilities were extended to include two additional properties in Alton plus, of course, additional remuneration and expenses.

Once a month, I would visit my Area manager for discussion about my properties. From time to time, I attended briefings organized by Hanover headquarters on policy and various developments. These occasions provided a welcome opportunity to meet other Housing managers and discuss topics of mutual interest.

Maintaining a positive dialogue with residents was a primary responsibility in the interests of ensuring satisfaction. Complaints were not unusual, but resolving them was straightforward and satisfying. The residents were from a wide range of society, and individual attention with discretion was necessary.

While continuing my role with Wiltshire County Council, Sue accepted a transfer from Ministry of Defence Army to a Royal Navy establishment at Topsham, in Devon. A consequence of this was my retirement from the County Council and our relocating from Collingbourne Ducis.

Having acquired an Exmoor pony from Wendy Vint in Wootton Courtenay,

Andover Advertiser – 20 March 1992

Ex-tra sad farewell

HARRY Crawford is a man with a past.

He is an ex-county councillor, ex-parish clerk, ex-chairman of the village show committee, ex-village hall trust treasurer and soon to be an ex-resident of Collingbourne Ducis.

Harry is to 'follow the drum' as he puts it, and move near Exeter where his wife, Sue — a mobile grade in the civil service — has recently been relocated.

After 15 years in the village the family is sad to leave but for Harry, after a 32-year army career with the Royal Engineers where he rose to the rank of Lt-Col, upping roots is not too much of a trial.

He spent many years as an almost integral part of the community and particularly enjoyed his time on Wiltshire County Council where for the last year he held the prestigious position of vice-chairman of the council.

Co-ordinating a training organisation for 40 local farms, arranging talks and courses and working as part-time local management representative for the Hanover Housing Association has kept him busy in recent years.

Harry is not quite sure what he will be doing in Exeter but says he will not be going 'mouldy'.

There is one member of the family who is particularly pleased to be taking the trip further West.

He is Mouse, Sue's young Exmoor pony.

"There is an old saying that Exmoor ponies always go home, but I did not bargain on our pony going home so soon, and taking us with him," said Harry.

Re-locating to the West Country 1992.

and bearing in mind that Exmoor ponies often return to their native moor, we found ourselves considering properties on or around Exmoor. In due course, our offer for The Dell, a four-bedroom farmhouse in Timberscombe, was accepted. While I arranged the sale of our cottage, I stayed in her mother's adjacent cottage while Sue stayed in a comfortable B&B in Topsham during the working week.

We then sold mother-in-law's cottage and moved to The Dell in 1991, with the contents of both cottages.

– 25 –
The Riding for the Disabled Association
Porlock

When we moved to Timberscombe, West Somerset, the local chairman of the Parish Council called to say there was a vacancy and asked if I would consider being involved. I declined, firstly, because our move to The Dell was quite complicated with domestic tasks. Secondly, the last thing I wanted as a new resident was to become involved in local politics. The chairman of the Conservative Party's local committee was the next to approach me. I declined again. There followed an impassioned appeal from Wendy Vint, who had introduced Sue to Exmoor ponies, persuading me to help the Porlock Branch of the Riding for the Disabled Association RDA. It needed a secretary. I said I would give the matter some thought, but in the same moment realised that I could not easily decline, such was the quite long-standing relationship between our families and remembering the party she had arranged for us during which we met a lot of local people. I agreed to offer myself for the appointment, met the chairman and her committee, and was elected in a matter of minutes.

I attended a few riding sessions to get a feel for RDA activities and spent a while with the treasurer, who told me about the financial situation and the way in which the Branch was administered. Committee meetings took place roughly on a monthly basis, and I used to meet the chairman prior to each meeting tro draw up an agenda for circulation.

Bar the treasurer and myself, the committee comprised ladies, one of whom was Chief Instructor and a well-qualified horse-woman. As well as taking the minutes, I played a full part in the discussions that took place about policy, fund-raising activities, and the general operation of the Branch, which I came to realise was in very good shape financially and every other way. It was a happy, contented group, free from adverse interaction.

An essential requirement was the recruitment of helpers. They were needed to manage the riding activities and have an appreciation of individual disabilities. They would have to supervise individual riders, who usually needed assistance and encouragement. Helpers had responsibility for safety.

During the six years while I was secretary, the recruitment of suitable helpers became increasingly difficult. People just couldn't afford the time and some who might have helped responded badly to the rider's difficulties. The helpers I had known began to fall away, mainly on account of age. There came a time when we had to consider disbanding the Branch. When this possibility became known at RDA Headquarters there was mention of the Branch's funds being transferred to HQ. This was firmly resisted by the committee, bearing in mind that the substantial balance in our bank account represented a great deal of hard work on fund-raising activities. As the situation was coming to a head we agreed, as a committee, that the existing fund should be transferred to the Taunton Branch of the RDA, and that happened before HQ could interfere. The Branch was disbanded and HQ informed.

– 26 –
The Exmoor Tourist Association
Somerset

Tourism is an important contributor to the local economy in West Somerset. The Exmoor Tourist Association (ETA) was formed in 1977 to provide for proprietors of Bed & Breakfast and Self Service accommodation a corporate body to advertise and promote tourism on Exmoor. In the 1990's, the membership comprised some 250 businesses. I became a member in 1993, when I launched our own B&B business at The Dell in Timbescombe.

At that time, tourism was managed by the ETA, the West Somerset District Council (WSDC), and the Exmoor National Park Authority (ENPA). The three organisations staged a meeting annually, and all interested businesses were invited to attend. The meeting was addressed by the ETA chairman, the WSDC chairman, and the ENPA Officer. They reviewed the status of tourism referring to statistical information, developments that had taken place, and proposals for the future. An open forum followed during which delegates had an opportunity to respond, to ask questions, and to raise issues concerning their businesses. It was a useful occasion, when a wide range of points of view were expressed in the interests of promoting tourism in the Exmoor area.

During the 1998 ETA AGM it was announced that the chairman had moved out of the area and resigned, and the nomination of a replacement was needed. There was no response from the members. During the 1999, AGM the need for a chairman was repeated without success. In 2000, the acting chairman circulated to the membership a note requesting earnest consideration be given to the vacancy for chairman, adding that in the absence of a nomination the committee would have to consider disbanding the association.

It seemed to me that disbandment was a serious and unnecessary threat and should be avoided at all costs. I contacted the acting chairman and requested an opportunity to discuss the matter and was minded to volunteer for the chairmanship. He welcomed my offer and went on to explain the composition of the committee, the allocation of responsibilities, finance, current issues, and the administrative routine in force. At the end of our discussion, I confirmed my offer which, it was agreed, would be put to the membership at the forthcoming 2000 AGM. My nomination was accepted and I was appointed chairman.

In 2001, the Tourism Officer at WSDC took upon himself to propose a merger of tourism in West Somerset with tourism in North Devon. The Exmoor area straddled both authorities. This initiative was rejected and the Tourism Officer resigned. Concerned about the way forward, chairman WSDC convened a meeting of the principal people in the tourist industry, which was attended by chairman ETA (myself) and representatives of various other splinter groups, e.g. the Minehead Hoteliers, the Porlock Tourist Association, the Farm Holiday Group, Butlins, Watchet Tourism Group, and a few others. As a result of that meeting, we decided to form a Tourism Forum of all the principals involved in the industry, co-chaired by chairman WSDC, the representative of the Farm Holiday Group, and we would meet on a monthly basis.

On reporting this major change to the ETA committee, there was an immediate adverse reaction. The previously predominant role of the ETA in tourism, together with WSDC, and ENPA, seemed under threat. For many years, the ETA in co-operation with WSDC (as a source of funding), had published the Tourism Guide, in which interested businesses advertised their services and the attractions for holiday makers. During a meeting of the Forum, it was proposed that the traditional mention of the ETA on the front cover be discontinued since the content and publication of the guide would in future be the responsibility of the Forum.

The ETA committee saw this as a further demonstration of efforts to diminish the role of the ETA. Concurrently with the Forum, a Tourism Consortium of representatives of the various business groups met regularly to monitor the proceedings of the Forum and to prepare proposals for forthcoming meetings; the difference between the Forum and the Consortium being that WSDC was not represented on the Consortium.

The reorganisation of the management of tourism compared with the arrangments pre-2001 was bitterly opposed by the ETA. I continued to attend meetings of the Forum in order to keep up-to-date with developments. With the agreement of the ETA committee, I resigned from the Consortium where the proceedings became political, and the ETA was barely recognised.

Exmoor was one of the areas severely affected by the national Foot and Mouth crisis. As a precaution to prevent the spread of the disease to the deer herd, all public paths in the National Park were closed. Farms were required to provide facilities at accesses for the disinfection of footwear. The restrictions published in the national press created the impression that Exmoor itself was 'closed', and that inevitably resulted in an absence of visitors. Businesses depending on tourism for income were very seriously affected.

The ETA was aware of the distress being felt by many proprietors of B&B and Self-Service businesses who relied on income from tourism. The government, anxious to provide financial assistance, made provision through Regional Development agencies (RDAs) throughout the UK. Following my approach to the RDA in Bristol, on behalf of ETA, business representatives came to the Moorland Hall at Wheddon Cross to meet members and discuss financial difficulties.

I attended the meeting to see how things were going. There were many people in the hall. The official in charge explained to me that the RDA could not simply dish out money however deserving a case might be. It was necessary to see accounts and evidence of business performance preceding the Foot and Mouth crisis. It had become apparent during the morning that few of those requesting assistance kept acceptable accounts nor were they able to demonstrate past performance. While identifying many cases of difficulty, the RDA was unable to assist in a majority of those cases.

The ENPA convened regular meetings when the up-to-date foot and mouth crisis in the Exmoor area was considered. It was during these meetings that I was able to represent the concerns of ETA members, but there was little that could be done while the restrictions on movement continued to apply.

The previous matter of the merger with the North Devon authority was raised almost continuously. The ETA, being firmly opposed, adopted a 'Stand Alone' position, and this was well supported to such an extent that the proposal was eventually dropped.

An important annual occasion was the 'Leaflet Exchange', when all interested parties met to promote their enterprises by taking a table at which promotional material was readily available. Organised by the ETA for all-comers, this was a popular event attended by a wide range of businesses involved in tourism in the widest sense of the word.

Although I enjoyed my role as chairman ETA and was blessed with a committee of enthusiastic and hard-working members, it seemed wrong to me to continue indefinitely. I gave six months notice of my intention to resign and asked the committee to start finding a replacement. As the months passed, I reminded the committee at each meeting because nothing seemed to be happening about a new chairman. At the last committee meeting, I resigned and noted that my position would be vacant. I concluded that it was thought I would continue in post!

On the date set for the next committee meeting, I approached Anthony Brunt, the proprietor of the Yarn Market hotel in Dunster, who was an ETA member, saying I had been trying to find a successor without success. He asked me to tell him what was involved, which I did. At the end of my briefing, he said he would have a go at it. I said: the next committee meeting is at 2.00 pm this afternoon! He said 'I will be there!' I phoned the secretary and asked her to let committee members know.

Shortly afterwards, the Forum of principal people managing tourism was renamed 'Visit Exmoor' with a secretary in an office in Dulverton. Yet another reorganization took place, but it ran into troubled times with much infighting and was eventually replaced with 'The Exmoor Tourism Partnership' of core organisations. An Exmoor Tourism Conference was held each autumn providing an opportunity for the sector to meet together, share best practice, learn of new initiatives, network, and develop training and products. The present chairman (2016) was a member of my ETA committee back in 2000.

Since 2000, the management of tourism on Exmoor has bounced from one form to another, each set-up trying to bring together everyone concerned for the future, but suffering the effects of destructive competitive attitudes along the way. Through all of this, the ETA has retained its reputation contributing continuously to the well-being of tourism in the South West. I am glad to have belonged to the ETA as a member and subsequently as its chairman for six years.

– 27 –
Our Exmoor Pony Enterprise

Our association with Exmoor ponies started at a dinner party where we met Wendy Vint, a well-known local breeder, of Riverside Farm, Wootton Courtenay. Wendy invited Sue to visit Riverside Farm when she was next in the area. As a result of that meeting, we acquired our first Exmoor filly foal and joined the Exmoor Pony Society (EPS). Dunkery Titmouse (AKA Mouse) got off to a splendid start as a yearling by winning first place at Exford Show.

We went to the show from our home in Wiltshire for the fun of it, not thinking for a minute that Mouse would distinguish herself so early in her life. In the same year, she was second at Dunster Show and Best Yearling. As a two-year old, she was reserve champion at the Bath & West Show. In 2000, she was reserve champion at Dunster Show, and her foal was Best Foal, the sire being the well-known Ice Cream, of the famous Anchor Herd.

As reserve champion she qualified for the Exmoor Pony of the year competition and was Best Mare. In the same year, she was shown at five other shows, taking first place in all of them. That was the pinnacle of her career. Mouse had become a well-known, well-bred, and very successful pony.

We started our enterprise with 4 acres bought from farmer Tommy Heard. After a couple of years, and with a growing herd, Tommy persuaded Sue to buy the remaining 9½ acres of his Pitfield. Buying at £2k per acre and selling at £10k per acre in 2014 proved a very sound investment. Having bought the field, we set about dividing it into six paddocks, supplying water to each paddock and employing contractors to erect post and wire fencing throughout.

During our showing and breeding programme we had fifteen Exmoor ponies on our 13½ acre Pitfield. At the same time, I had a Dales pony, Henry, and Sue had a Fell pony, Gillie, both of them broken to saddle and shown successfully locally and at Penrith in Cumbria. Gillie subsequently produced two beautiful foals. Sue and I rode our ponies Mouse and Henry over Exmoor on many happy and adventurous occasions, but our primary interest was showing and breeding.

I recall an occasion when riding my Dales pony, Henry, outside the collecting ring in which I would shortly show him. I was approached by a lady very fashionably dressed in country tweeds and a large hat. She asked why my pony was wearing coloured ribbons on his tail. I explained that the Dales and Fells ponies though quite different in the eyes of those experienced weren't

OUR EXMOOR PONY ENTERPRISE

Harry and Sue set off for a ride over the moor.

Donkey 'Dora' leading the procession on Palm Sunday.

easily identified by others. In order to demonstrate the difference the Fell Society had agreed that Dales ponies should wear ribbons. She thanked me, saying my explanation was most interesting.

A few minutes later, my class was called into the ring. After the traditional walk, trot, and canter round the ring, I presented Henry to the judge for his individual assessment. The judge greeted me saying "Well, well – we meet again." She was the lady who had enquired about ribbons!

Harry learning to drive.

Harry on his Dales pony 'Henry'.

Sue introduced the Fell ponies to the Dunster Show to replace a class that had been withdrawn through lack of support. While she was showing Jack, one of Gillie's progeny in the Fell ring, the Exmoor championship was called, and Mouse was eligible. Sue had shown her to first place in her class earlier. As Sue was tied up in the Fell ring, I had to show Mouse in the championship, although I had retired from showing a couple of years previously. Anyway,

The bridge to our field built by Harry.

Mouse was awarded Reserve Champion. As is customary, the champion and the reserve champion did a lap of honour. On stepping into a trot with Mouse I said to her "Let's make a good job of this" and promptly measured my length on the deck!

With my hands under my body I couldn't get up but was immediately surrounded by willing hands, all belonging to ladies! Along came our great friend Derek Sparks, who managed Captain Ronnie Wallace's Anchor herd. He bent down to my level and unhelpfully said, "You should have given up this business a long time ago" before lifting me up. I didn't show ever again!

At Dunster Show, in 2010, one of Mouse's foals, Cowbridge Spring Water (AKA Spring) hit the headlines by coming first in the Exmoor four-year-old and over Class, then winning the Exmoor championship, and after lunch becoming Mountain and Moorland champion over all of the nine national native breeds.

We had started the day with Spring refusing to enter the trailer. After fifteen minutes or so, Sue was edging towards calling it a day but as had happened on many previous occasions, a pony will eventually give in, as was the case that morning with Spring. It was our most successful day of showing since Mouse excelled herself in 2000.

The 'Gathering' of the Exmoor pony herds at Winsford Hill (Anchor herd), at Brightworthy (Mitchell's herd) and on Dunkery Hill (Langdon/Ablett and Western herds) were annual occasions when mares and their foals were rounded up for registration as pure-bred ponies, subject to inspection. I used to help riding my Dales pony at Brightworthy and Dunkery Hill. About eight of us would be spaced out in a long line moving slowly forward and encouraging the ponies to congregate and move ahead as a group.

In the case of Brightworthy, we crossed the Barle at a ford. On Henry's first Gathering, he was a bit hesitant on facing the river, but step by step with a bit of heel and stick, he moved into the water. Where it got deep, up to my boots, he cleverly turned to present his rump to the flow before dashing onto the bank. He didn't hesitate on future occasions!

Henry was canny about the terrain. Once while trying to catch up with the other riders beyond the Barle, I attempted a shortcut. We came on an area of bright green grass. Henry stopped, recognizing the area as a bog, and forced me to choose another route!

Susan on Dunkery Titmouse.    *Susan on Fell pony 'Gillie'.*

Susan with Dunkery Titmouse and her foal.

By 2013, we were running out of energy and managing our stock during very wet and windy winters was taking its toll. I had stopped showing and was unable to assist Sue as I had done. Furthermore, we were finding the handling of ponies increasingly hazardous. The 2014 winter was particularly bad with the pasture a sea of mud. Working with the ponies and feeding them standing in mud, with wind, rain, and everything else that nature could throw at her, Sue decided she could not face another Exmoor winter. We then had to consider reducing our stock.

Selling was one option and homing ponies on loan was another. In two cases, we sold successfully but offering ponies on loan as, for instance, companions was not successful, and in any case, we didn't like the prospect of our ponies ending their lives in uneventful retirement.

The last option and the least desirable was to have ponies put down. After much heart-aching we had Gillie put down at Potters' abattoir. Although the job was done very efficiently by sympathetic chaps, it was a thoroughly unpleasant experience and one, we decided, would not be repeated. With three other ponies to dispose of before winter, Rob Blomfield-Richards who had bought Pitfield, and generously allowed our remaining ponies to continue to live there, went a generous step further by arranging for a JCB to dig a large pit in the field, where all of our ponies had spent their lives. We then arranged for Richard, the Kennel Huntsman, to shoot the three of them. We were not present but Rob and Phil Bassett, who undertook to manage the disposal, said afterwards that there was absolutely no distress such was Richard's expertise with his rifle and at the end the ponies, wearing head collars and rosettes, were at peace as if asleep.

Thus came to an end some twenty-five years of a hugely enjoyable enterprise.

In the following year, our dachshund Martha produced seven lovely puppies. Six were sold to very nice owners and one, named Centenary Poppy, was kept. Sue felt if she could no longer participate in pony rings, she would try her hand showing dachshunds!

Susan with foal 'Cowbridge Leat'.

– 28 –
The Exmoor Pony Society
Somerset

We became members of the Exmoor Pony Society on the outset of our interest and gradually became acquainted with all and sundry. AGMs were well attended and the agenda usually attracted lots of speakers both for and against the various items. Occasionally differences of opinion necessitated a vote. AGMs were fairly lively occasions.

In 1998 I was invited to stand for election to the committee. Following the standard procedure of finding a proposer and a seconder and submitting my name, I was duly elected.

One thing I found unusual was the procedure whereby the voting papers for the annual election of committee members were returned to the secretary. With the support of a few committee members, Derek Sparks elected sometime later than myself included, and some ordinary members, I raised the matter at an AGM submitting that the voting process should be administered by an independent person. For the next election voting papers were returned to the Exmoor National Park Authority officer who subsequently informed the chairman of the result.

The UK was divided into various areas with an Area Representative appointed to communicate with members and to organize events, particularly during the winter months when there would otherwise not be much going on. The County of Somerset was an area looked after by Yvonne Campbell. The committee decided that Exmoor within Somerset deserved its own area.

Sue and I were appointed representatives. We organized very popular winter events, e.g. Antique evenings at the Moorland Hall in Wheddon Cross. Members were invited to bring an antique which was examined by Luke Macdonald of Lawerences Auctioneers, and its origin and purpose, if necessary, were explained and value suggested. Some very unusual and interesting items were valued. A light supper was included in the entrance fee. Following the first such occasion we happened to meet Luke in Taunton and asked him if he would like to deal with another similar event. "Oh, yes," he said, adding that we would be surprised at the number of items entered in sales as a result of our evenings.

On one occasion, an elderly lady member presented an attractive plate which Luke duly examined. Before suggesting a value, he turned it over to see on the back 'Microwave Safe'!

Other popular events were darts competitions in various pubs, talks on various equine topics at the Moorland Hall, and an annual dinner with a speaker.

During the spring and autumn, we organized enjoyable rides over the moor, also very popular.

As Area Representatives, Sue and I were allowed to attend committee meetings as observers so that we could keep our members informed about on-going matters.

I kept a simple account of the money raised from events, which was ploughed back in payment for speakers and the subsidizing of catering at events. The account was examined annually by member Peter Farmer and a copy endorsed 'Approved' was passed to the treasurer.

Creenagh Mitchell managed a 'Friend's of Exmoor Ponies' stall at shows raising as much as £1000 annually, which was passed to the treasurer at the AGM. The committee decided to commission the construction of a large trailer unit which was subsequently used for the display of promotional material and for the sale of goods by the Friend's initiative, which went up market under the control of Jackie Ablett and Gill Langdon. They were very dedicated to the success of the business, attending many local shows.

– 29 –
The Moorland Mousie Trust

The Moorland Mousie Trust is a charity set up by Valerie Sherwin with the objective of providing a centre where visitors to Exmoor could see ponies at close quarters and where unwanted ponies, mostly male, could avoid being put down. Prior to that initiative visitors often missed seeing the ponies. Running free on the moor they can conceal themselves very easily.

Valerie Sherwin's enterprise was supported by the National Park, with quite generous funding. She was able to acquire a barn surplus to requirements and worked very hard with volunteers to create what ultimately became the Exmoor Pony Centre. Sue Baker, one of the most knowledgeable people about the ponies, who wrote the well-known publication *Survival of the Fittest*, also had plans for a pony centre and had formed a small steering committee to develop her dream. However, Sue's proposals didn't enjoy funding to quite the same extent as the Sherwin enterprise. Eventually the development of the Sherwin project advanced to near completion while the Baker aspiration alas gradually foundered.

Valerie Sherwin, needing administrative and physical support, contacted a number of friends, acquaintances, and a National Park representative, asking them to meet with her to discuss the future of the pony centre scheme. Sue, myself, and a few others including a National Park representative agreed to help her and a more formal meeting was convened to discuss how we might help.

The upshot of that meeting was the adoption of my suggestion that a company should be formed, and I proceeded to do just that with Companies House. That entailed forming a board and those of us then involved agreed to be board members; Sue and myself, Katherine McKenzie (retired lawyer), Mary Hannah (pony owner and breeder), John Allan (farmer), and Valerie Sherwin. At the next meeting, we considered the matter of appointing a chairman and agreed to take it in turns to chair meetings. This became so unsatisfactory with regard to drafting agendas and the taking of minutes that my offer to be chairman on a regular basis was accepted unanimously. The next requirement was to appoint a secretary. Following the advertising of the position, Sue Crawford and two other board members sat together as an interviewing panel, met the applicants, and made a selection. The National Park Development fund had been providing finance against a total grant all of which had not been drawn. Kate McKenzie and I met the National Park official in charge of the fund at my house to discuss the drawing down of the outstanding grant. It transpired that each payment had to be justified in detail and a case would need to be made for the remaining grant which amounted to some thousands of pounds. Kate and I put to the fund manager a justification for the final payment, which was accepted verbally but subject to a formal presentation in writing. We prepared the written justification, which boiled down to the works necessary for the completion of the Centre, and the remaining grant was released.

Once the Centre was completed, visitors hired the ponies and enjoyed riding them over the moor under the supervision of qualified leaders. Additionally, Taster Sessions were arranged for youngsters and other inexperienced visitors. Once the fees for these activities had been settled, John Allan and I met at his house in Cornwall to draft a projection of income and expenditure for the next twelve months. Thereafter, the actual proceeds and expenses incurred were compared with the projection at board meetings and a satisfactory financial situation was confirmed.

An important item on an agenda was the need for a patron. Valerie considered Johnny Kingdom, a local naturalist and publisher, a suitable candidate. He had supported her on a few live TV interviews. The rest of us thought we needed a better known personality. I suggested Camilla, Duchess of Cornwall. Although a popular suggestion the chances of success seemed remote. I contacted the local Conservative Constituency office for advice about the correct way to address the Duchess and a suitable single A4 page letter was drafted for Valerie's signature. I think we were a bit taken aback on receiving an acceptance from Clarence House.

The Duchess would be happy to be patron for a period of five years. Promotional material, letterheads, etc., were suitably amended.

Mary Hannah and I attended a one-day course on fund-raising in Taunton. It was explained to us that all of the major charities in the UK were obliged to dispose of some assets every year and that the amount disposed of in the current year was £1.2 million. I purchased a reference book entitled "Charities in the UK" in which we found listed details of every charity together with information about activities that they supported and those they did not support. We were advised to study the book and select charities that seemed to favour livestock management, ponies in particular, and associated topics. Having shot off a few applications, we were encouraged on receiving several cheques for significant amounts of money.

An important outlet for ponies taken in by the trust was the opportunity to place them in various parts of the UK for conservation grazing. This was arranged by Juliet Rogers (Valerie's co-founder and trustee).

Sadly, personality differences meant that the development of the Moorland Mousie Trust was not always easy or happy, and it was insufficiently recognised that what it was possible to do in managing an enterprise of this type as an individual could not properly be done when there was company status and a board of directors. In the end, six of the board members gave notice of their resignation followed by myself, but not before I had informed Companies House and the Charity Commission.

Another influence in the local pony fraternity was Dawn Westcott, recently married to Nick Westcott, a well-known local farmer. Dawn has sometimes made controversial statements but she does know about the training of horses and Exmoor ponies in particular. Dawn and Nick formed a new organization namely The Moorland Exmoor Pony Breeders Group (MEPBG), recruiting members and expounding their own views about the protection of the Exmoor breed, conservation grazing, and just about every aspect of breed promotion.

We thus had the EPS, the MMT and now the MEPBG all competing for prominence in the business of promoting the Exmoor pony breed and in their own ways proving successful. We attended the first MEPBG show with a couple of ponies to demonstrate non-partisan interest but also to see how many members of the EPS were prepared to raise their heads above the parapet! The judge, well known to us, was Rex Milton of a very famous family with historical links to the Exmoor breed.

The Moorland Mousie Trust and Centre are now under new management and are thriving. Relationships, once frosty with the Exmoor Pony Society, have improved greatly and it has been a pleasure to see the Exmoor Pony Society trailer and the Moorland Mousie Trust stand side-by-side at shows.

– 30 –
Downsizing

During 2007, we were finding our five-bedroomed home unnecessarily large, and the maintenance of the garden, the paddock, and the outbuildings a bit of an over burden. We decided to downsize before it was too late, due to age.

We wanted to remain in Timberscombe but didn't know of an alternative property that would suit us. Towards the end of the year we were invited to a party in a bungalow in Great House Street. Our hostess gave her guests a conducted tour of the property. On the way home we agreed that the Pondside bungalow was the place for us!

The next day, we discovered who owned it and that our hostess of the night before was a tenant. During the church garden party, I met Judith Ford, who with her husband, Trevor, owned the bungalow and the house he had built next door. I explained our interest and our wish to purchase the bungalow. As the existing tenancy had twelve months to run, we had plenty of time to dispose of our home at The Dell but the tenants had a bust-up with the Fords with the result that the bungalow became available much earlier.

We placed The Dell on the market in 2008, sold it in sixteen weeks for a top of the market figure, and bought Pondside.

– 31 –
Farming

We had a flock of 40 Black Welsh Mountain sheep at Pitfield, as well as our ponies. We started with six ewes, bought a ram, and registered our little flock with the Breed Association based in Brecon. We then joined a once-a-week sheep husbandry course to learn how to look after our sheep and about breeding. Our first lambing was quite successful in spite of very cold weather. One of the ewes produced twins but rejected one of her lambs which, brought home, recovered in the Rayburn and was bottle fed for a few days before being accepted by another ewe.

Some of our black Welsh Mountain sheep.

As time passed, our flock increased to a mixed herd of forty 'boys' and 'girls'. Bill Liversage, a local farmer, and Bertram Sample, a retired farmer, gave

Winter woes.

FARMING

Spring feeding.

Summer feeding.

The white interloper!

us great advice. Bill had his own small licensed abattoir to which we took our ram lambs for slaughter. Bill shot them very humanely, stripped them of their fleeces and cut up the carcasses into joints and chops etc., which we stored in our deep freeze. The fleeces were cured for us and sold quite successfully as black and white rugs to B&B guests. As the quantity of meat increased, we sold that locally at a price a little below what butcher Gerald David was charging in Minehead. The meat became very popular and with the sale of fleeces we were making a profit on the whole enterprise.

One year, with virtually no experience of showing sheep, we decided to take half a dozen sheep to the Brecon Show and auction. On arrival, our sheep were inspected in the trailer. Two of them failed inspection on account of horns not being quite right. These were not allowed to leave the trailer. The other four were placed in a pen in a shed where a great many Black Welsh sheep enthusiasts were busy brushing and combing their sheep in readiness for the show. What a happy lot of people. Aware that we were not very experienced our neighbours generously gave us a few tips as we prepared our own sheep.

The judging was in two places, one for ewe lambs and another for the ram lambs. Sue dealt with the ewes, while I joined a long line of men and women showing ram lambs. Standing in the sunshine, I noticed that all the sheep being shown were jet black whereas mine was dark brown! I mentioned this to the chap next door who smiled saying "my ram lamb has been inside for the past couple of weeks and I expect yours has been out in the weather" Quite right, says I, with a lesson learnt! Along came the judge who on his hunkers eyeing my ram lamb looked up at me with an expression suggesting "We've got a right one here", meaning me, of course, rather than my ram. As the judge proceeded along the row I asked my friend what was wrong with that. Says he, "You must have a three finger space between the horns". Second lesson learnt. I quickly concluded that we had best concentrate on showing ponies!

We also had Call ducks on the leat at The Dell, and half a dozen hens in the summer house converted to a hen house. One of the hens sat on a few duck eggs. When hatched the hen went crazy as the ducklings shot off to the water! We had our fair share of fox trouble from time to time. Following one incident, when all the hens were killed and only one taken, I set up one of the dead hens with its head tied with thread to the open trap door in such a way that the next fox attacking the hen would brake the thread, close the trap door and find itself confined to the hen house.

The next morning, I noticed from a distance that the trap door was shut and assumed that the fox was in the hen house. Not a bit of it, on closer examination, I found a couple of feet of tongued and grooved timber wall missing. The fox had escaped!

We built our own hay shed with capacity for about three hundred small bales. When more bales were made, the excess was stored outside on pallets and under sheeting. However carefully we tied down the sheets, the winter

Our hens.　　　　　　　　　　　*Sue cares for a hen.*

FARMING

Hay making.

weather crept in. Wet bales are heavy and burning them had to be postponed until they dried out.

Hay was made on two of our six paddocks: about 5 acres in all. Most years we made about three hundred small bales. By applying fertilizer every three of four years, we could make as much as eight hundred small bales. Bill Liversage's son, Russell, made the hay initially but he didn't have an eight bale 'collector' so the bales were scattered all over the place and had to be collected individually and stacked on our trailer, which was hard work.

George Winter and his daughter, Susie, used to turn up unexpectedly, having seen the baler at work from their bedroom window. They helped collect the bales and store them in the shed. George could carry two bales at a time! Latterly we got contractor Chris Sully to make the hay. He had all the equipment, stored the bales in the hay shed and bought any surplus above our needs. The net cost to us worked out at about 27p per bale which was very satisfactory since bought-in bales cost about £2.50 or more each on the open market.

We built a fine pony shelter with two bays each 12 feet square. The ponies lived out all year round but had the option of shelter in the winter and shade in the summer. After about ten

Hay turned prior to baling.

years the shelter started to fall apart so we replaced it with two fine stables, each 12 by 12 feet on 8 inches of concrete, supplied and constructed by Barry Fowler. One of these was useful for excess hay when we had it and for bedding straw. The sheep enjoyed shelter in half-moon arcs bought from Mole Valley Farmers.

By 2014 I didn't have the energy to assist Sue as I had done previously. Erecting sheep/pony proof fencing done by myself for years was contracted out to Derek Robinson. We agreed that Sue could no longer be expected to face the wind, the mud and the rain thrown at us during the winter months and decided reluctantly to dispose of our livestock before the 2015 winter, consisting then of six ponies and Dora our donkey. We sold one, had four put down and were fortunate to have one Exmoor and the donkey accepted by the Donkey Sanctuary in Sidmouth.

Pitfield, bought in 2000 for £ 2000 an acre, was sold in 2014 for £10,000 an acre. With bank interest rates low at 0.5% we decided to invest the proceeds in a new-build two bedroomed terrace house in College Gardens, Alcombe, near Minehead thus drawing to a close our twenty-two years breeding and showing ponies and our a small flock of sheep. We found a tenant for the house in Alcombe quickly and found £600 pcm altogether more satisfactory than the bank interest then just £17 per month.

Epilogue

Change has always appealed to me during a career punctuated by changes of place, the nature of the work, and the people with whom the work has been done. Sometimes, decisions were taken for me, but at other times there were alternative options that were not sufficiently explored.

Foremost in the latter category were firstly, my marriage, too early and to the wrong person. Wives had a role to play in service life, and I believe, to a much greater extent than in any other profession. The wives of successful seniors I have known were committed and dedicated to the responsibilities of their husbands. Indeed, one or two wives I knew well did a better job than their spouses! Secondly, my management of the reorganisation of UK representation in the United States could have been better. Thirdly, the turmoil of divorce, undoubtedly had a detrimental effect on my career prospects in the Army.

While considering the Long Survey course, I considered also leaving the Army altogether. I paid my godfather, George Palmer, a visit to discuss my situation. His conclusion was that my attention had become unduly focused on far horizons, at the expense of day-to-day matters. His analogy was as follows: "I used to like watching cricket and one day, when the village XI was short of a man, the Captain asked me to play. I was no cricketer but he insisted that I help him out. From that moment, I was determined to remain on the village team, concentrating in the nets and watching the skill of the others. In due course, I became a County player."

It was sound advice from a man who having started as a clerk in the Friends' Provident and Century Insurance Company's Howard Street office in Belfast rose to become the Company's Chief Executive in London.

A really terrible error of judgement was choosing the Sun Life of Canada on retirement from the Army, instead of a more secure occupation with the railway. The latter, I subsequently discovered, being open to retired Royal Engineer Lieutenant-Colonels. Moreover, my father and grandfather, having been railway people, would undoubtedly have strengthened my application.

Instead of accepting positions with the Agricultural Training Board and Hanover Housing, both enjoyable but not attracting an adequate salary, Sue and I should have started a business. We were not able to start our very successful Bed & Breakfast business until we had moved from Collingbourne Ducis to Timberscombe.

While researching the many tributes paid to my father and his exceptional courage during the war, I like to think that my education and my career considerations suffered badly having been denied his influence and advice.

The title *Never Look Back* reflects a greater degree of rational thinking, resulting in greater success. But that is hindsight. I find myself looking back far too often and the effect can be extremely upsetting. What's done is done!

Everyone faces crossroads in their lives and decisions have to be made. The trouble is that the past catches up unexpectedly and presents problems already dealt with.

Time cannot erase the sadnesses of life, but it can help us to learn from them the hardest lesson of all: that even one's mistakes can be enriching.